R.J. Stewart
Biography

R.J. Stewart is a Scottish author, composer and musician living in the USA, wherein he was admitted in 1997 as a "Resident Alien of Extraordinary Ability," a category awarded to those with the highest achievements in the arts or sciences.

He has 41 books in publication worldwide, translated into many languages, and has recorded a wide range of music and meditational CDs, plus music for film, television, and theater productions in Britain, Canada, and the USA.

He teaches workshops and classes worldwide, has appeared in numerous films and documentaries, and gives concerts of his original music and songs, featuring the unique 80-stringed concert Psaltery and other instruments.

In 1988 R.J. Stewart founded the *Inner Temple Traditions InnerConvocation*™® program, which consists of a series of ongoing classes, publications, groups, and trained teachers working with spiritual and imaginative themes.

For further information, please visit the Stewart websites:

www.dreampower.com
www.rjstewart.org
www.rjstewart.net
www.innerconvocation.com

COPYRIGHT
R.J. Stewart © 2006

All rights reserved worldwide.
No part of this publication may be reproduced, stored
in any retrieval system or transmitted in any form or by any
means electronic mechanical photocopying recording or
otherwise without prior written permission from the author.
Contact: www.rjstewart.net.

Cover artwork and line drawings by Heather Brown
From designs by R.J. Stewart © 2006

Printed in the USA

A catalog record for this book is available
from the Library of Congress.

ISBN: 978-0-9791402-0-4

An Inner Temple Traditions InnerConvocation™® publication.

P.O. Box 7023
Boulder, CO 80306-7023
www.rjstewart.net

THE SPIRIT CORD

BY
R.J. STEWART

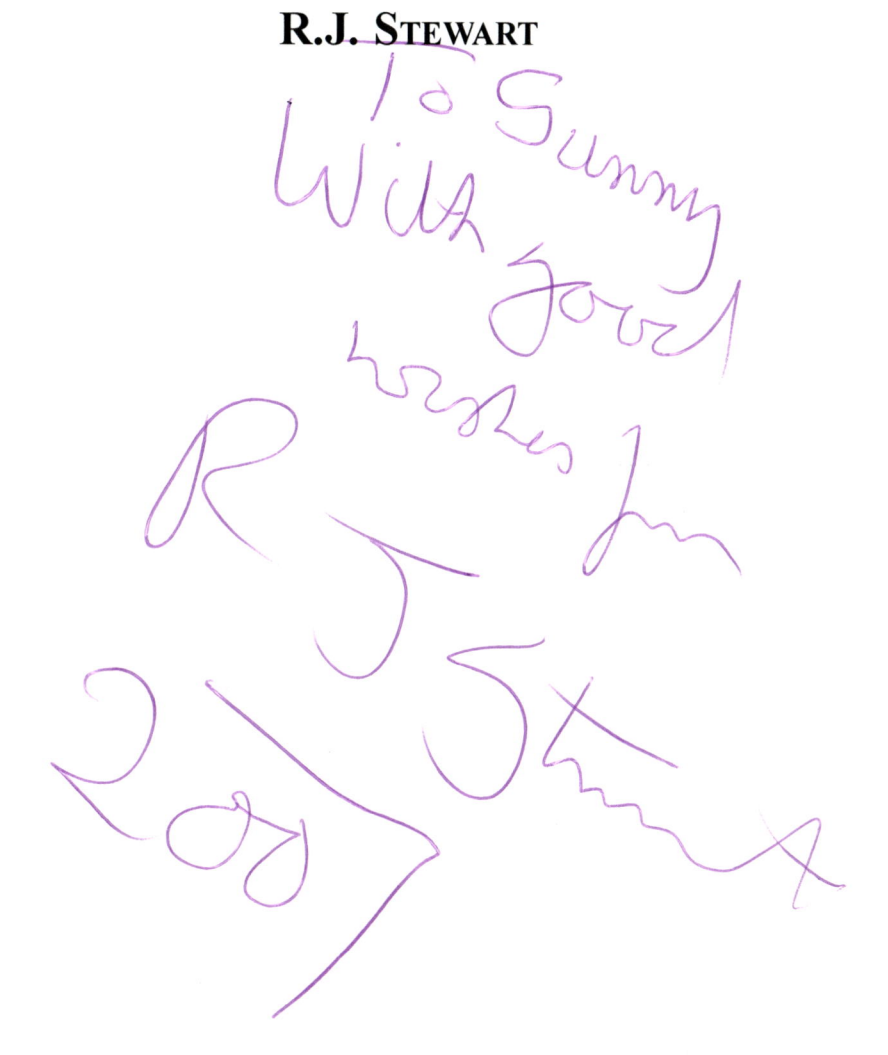

*To Sunny
With good
wishes from
RJ Stewart
2007*

Selected Titles
by R.J. Stewart

The Spiritual Dimension of Music
1987 Destiny Books, VT

Earth Light
1991 UK, and later US editions

Power Within the Land
1992 UK, and later US editions

Living Magical Arts
1985 UK (new 2006 edition Thoth Publications, UK)

The Miracle Tree
2003 New Page Books, NJ

The Well of Light
2004 Muse Press, FL

For a full list of all titles and recordings go to www.rjstewart.net which provides an online resource for mail order of R.J. Stewart's work and that of other authors and musicians. Please try your local bookstore first!

TABLE OF CONTENTS

Acknowledgements vi

Part One
    Introduction to Part One 1
1. Cord Forms 15
2. The Cord of Connection 23
3. The Twin Streams 31
4. The Astral Double of the Cord 43
5. Purifying the Imagination 55

Part Two
    Introduction to Part Two 69
6. Cord Positions 73
7. The Crossroads 81
8. The Temple of Dedication 91
9. The Lunar Realm 113
10. Further Cord Forms 131
11. The Cord of Death 141

Conclusion 153

Appendices
I. The Rivers of Blood and Tears 157
II. Orchil 175

Acknowledgements

Many books on spiritual or magical themes are written in theory only, but this one has been strongly shaped by practice. Substantial thanks are due to the many students and friends who worked with me in their Cord training during the series of workshops based on Spirit Cord material that began in 2001 and are still ongoing. Without their hands-on participation, their questions, comments, and shared experiences, I would not have been able to write this book in its present form, much of which derives from teaching and communicating the material directly to individuals and groups over several years and in many locations.

I would also like acknowledge Sherrie McCain-Kistler, who suggested writing **The Spirit Cord**, and whose support, friendship and astute comments on the manuscript, enabled the book that you now hold in your hands.

Jenny Stracke (Willow), for her work on copy-editing and formatting the book for publication, and her co-worker, Catherine Price.

Heather Brown, for the cover artwork and line drawings of the Cord positions.

An earlier version of the Crossroads material (Chapter 7) appeared in a different form in **The Well of Light**, the previous title in this series.

Figure 8, The Tree of Life, is by Jake Archer, adapted from a figure in my book **The Miracle Tree** (2002).

As always, I must acknowledge my spiritual mentors, visible and invisible, who set me upon the path and keep me upon it. They include, but are not limited to, W.G. Gray and Patricia Crowther who first introduced me to Cord magic in the 1970s, and A.R. Heaver, the Glastonbury adept. Nor should I forget the mysterious figure of transatlantic traveler and alchemist John Smythe (18th century) who recorded folkloric faery cord methods in his private notebooks.

R.J. Stewart
California, Winter 2006

PART ONE

Introduction to Part One

1. Cords and the Origins of Sacro-Magical Methods
2. Cord Magic Then, and Now
3. The Practical Cord Forms
4. In the Beginning: the Cord of the Mother
5. The Cord and Peg Demonstration
6. In the Middle: the Cord of Individuality
7. At the End: the Cord of Death
8. How to Use This Book

Cords and the Origins of Sacro-Magical Methods

Cords have been used in spiritual and magical practices for many thousands of years. Such a wide variety of usage, worldwide, past and present, would make a substantial and fascinating reference book. Practices range from cords used in many ways to bless or bind, to curse or liberate, to the knotted or plain ritual cords worn by specific orders or religions, to the widely known prayer beads (strung on a cord) of both Eastern and Western cultures. All such cord practices derive from ancient origins embodied in both folkloric magic and in spiritual and esoteric or mystical traditions. These deep roots are also embodied in numerous children's games with cords, especially those finger-weaving games that bring dexterity and flexibility. Many of these, patterns woven with a simple string between the fingers, have a magical or metaphysical significance which has been handed down in collective tradition through the centuries. Such patterns have repeatedly found their way into the more formal arenas of the temple, lodge, or dogmatic religion.

The Origins of Sacro-Magical Methods

While it was once thought that folkloric magic was the corrupt and ignorant remnant of formal practice descending either from formal religions or from ancestral sacro-magical practices to a lower common level as cultures changed. It is now amply clear that the reverse movement is what occurs. In other words, patterns of magic (of any kind) arise within the collective consciousness, and remain embodied there for many generations in folkloric magic. Such patterns developed, flourished, and were often intentionally systematized as so-called "higher" magic and as religious practices, and so remained present within formal religion. A living example of this synthesis that is well know today is found in the Tibetan Buddhist tradition. The Buddhist practices were grafted on to, but did not replace, the more ancient shamanistic techniques of the pre-evangelist period in Tibet. The result is a complex formal religion resting upon ancient folkloric sacro-magical foundations.

Such folkloric practices are always the foundation of the more formal practices. By folkloric we mean an anonymous tradition, with no known writer, founder, cult, sect, dogma or text, handed down in oral teaching and practice through the generations.

Another classic example, much discussed and studied, is that of the sacrificial and transubstantiation rituals of the ancestral world and of ancient cultures. These rituals still have parallels in primal or tribal rites today. Such practices, repeatedly amended yet retaining their central themes, became embodied at the core and heart of many formal religions, including Christianity. In Christianity these rituals became the Mass, Sacraments, Communion and so forth. Yet such rituals of mutual consumption and mutual absorption long predate Christianity. Christianity incorporated and combined the Jewish

Passover tradition with those of the death and consumption rituals of the Mediterranean Mystery cults.

In many cultures, especially during the Christian period, a formal religious veneer developed over the traditional practices. This veneer is sometimes a masking or protective process, and at other times the Christian element is taken and redefined within the older primal traditions, as can be seen in traditions such as Voudon or Santeria. This process allows people to go to Church (which they were often required to do by law, sometimes on pain of death), and continue to practice their real folkloric spiritual traditions without any conflict.

Cord Magic Then, and Now

Cord magic, or cord spirituality, is something that humans have always practiced in a wide variety of expressions and traditions. It is still found today at the most primal level in the folk magic of many cultures. This cord magic is often "hidden" in open view in the heart of the modern city and is by no means limited to remote regions and so-called "primitive" cultures.

Here, however, we are less concerned with folklore and more with practical use of the cord in contemporary spiritual and magical arts of transformation and as a tool for the exploration of consciousness. So while we refer, from time to time, to traditional sacro-magical arts involving cords, our main emphasis is on exercises and practices, on *forms*, for the present day.

The Practical Cord *Forms*

Throughout this book the word "forms" will be found: this is used to replace a motley collection of popular terms such as meditation, visualization, spiritual exercises, magical or physical techniques to change consciousness, and so forth. Many of the *forms* in our text combine several of the fore-going but some *forms* use none of them employing other methods of direct transformation of awareness through simple use of the physical cord itself. It is this direct quality that produces an immediate effect that is characteristic of spiritual and magical cord work. In later chapters, we will further explore the nature of *forms* that facilitate the power of the cord in our practical examples. Before doing so, we should first explore some of the basic concepts that are at the foundation of cord magic.

IN THE BEGINNING: THE CORD OF THE MOTHER

We are all born with a Cord…it connects us to our mother and nourishes us in the womb. This physical cord, like every part of the human organism, is the manifest form of a spiritual or inner connection. Such connections are more than individual or personal because they link the human, born in this world, to the greater consciousness of the cosmos which permeates many worlds. It is through this root concept of *connection* that the cord works for us and enables us to understand the principles of cord work in daily practice. At first we come to cord work as a somewhat abstract or theoretical concept of connection, but this concept is more than a merely intellectual or mental process…it embodies a principle of existence, a spiritual principle with direct physical attributes and effects.

The Cord embodies the principle of *that which connects*, and our primary cord meditation, based upon this concept, is both the most simple and most advanced form. A physical cord, be it a simple piece of string or a more elaborate ritual item, embodies and enables the principle of connection which flows through our cosmos at all levels of being.

Conversely, that same principle or law of *connection* gives us the Cord as a measure of *distance*, for by connecting between two points, it measures the distance that seems to separate them. Such principles of connection and separation, are made manifest in spiritual or magical practice through a physical cord. In daily life, such cords take a multitude of forms, from the nerves of the body to the power cords or cables of your computer system. But through intentional work with the principle of the Cord we establish a dedicated (physical) cord. The process is a gradual one, involving choosing or making a Cord, then working with it through several stages of expanding technique that substantially open out our awareness. We will return to this process in Chapter 1, and develop it throughout the book.

THE CORD AND PEG DEMONSTRATION

A classic example, and easily accessible demonstration is found in ancient philosophy and sacred geometry. This demonstration shows the inherent connective quality of the cord, and its relationship to the laws of Being, of Cosmos, which are expressed through many models of both physics and metaphysics. These qualities span from the ancestral to the most recent and contemporary. This simple practical demonstration involves the use of a cord and a peg. One end of the cord is fixed to the ground with the peg. If the other end is pulled and kept taut, and then you walk, there are only two directions you can go in, and only one shape that you can make. Try it!

This eminently practical Cord form is the basis of some powerful magic: if you do this as a daily discipline, and meditate upon its implications, your consciousness will expand and transform. This cord-and-peg, fixed-and-free, form is not a trivial exercise. It reveals something of the fundamental laws of shape and movement and the relationship between time and space through the inherent nature of the cord. We will return to this idea later and, in some of our practical examples, we will explore the way shapes can be made with the cord…shapes that change our consciousness.

The umbilical cord, without which we have no life, connects us to our mother and measures the distance that is created between the child and the mother. Once the child is born, and breathes the air of the outer world for the first time, the physical cord will gradually cease to function. In most modern cultures the umbilical cord is cut marking a dramatic entrance into outer life. This cutting is a formally enforced separation from the mother. However, there is still a cord of connection between child and mother which endures through many subtle levels of consciousness and energy. Both the physical umbilical cord and the subtle cord woven of psychic interaction and love are aspects of that metaphysical cord of Connection described above. Thus the birth and separation of humanity, individually and collectively, is defined by a cord of connection. That cord connects us to the greater consciousness of the cosmos, just as the umbilical and subtle cord of life connects us to the mother.

In the Middle: the Cord of Individuality

During our lifetime, we are supported and enabled by a cord. This is, of course, the spinal cord without which nothing could happen in our manifest existence. While the cord of the womb gave sustenance before separation, the cord of the spine gives individuality and operational potential, and the practical ability to move in the individual's separate and manifest life. The Cord of Individuality manifests with the spinal cord as a central core. From there it manifests through the many associated cords and connections of the body that all link into the spinal cord from which they receive their complex instructions that enable life to function in time, space, and movement. There is another aspect to this Cord of Individuality, which is transpersonal, and may arise over many lifetimes. We will return to this when we explore ideas about the Cord of Continuity, and the concept of *continuity between lives*. In this short preliminary outline we can recognize this transpersonal quality of intense individuality when we see, or live, dedicated lives that seem to have a strong direction, be it in arts, sciences, spirituality, or any other field of activity.

At the End: the Cord of Death

When we die, the manifest cord of the body, connecting the entire organism to the brain, ceases to function. Just as the birth cord and spinal cord embody and enable connection during the life, deriving from a greater principle of connection, so that principle asserts itself directly at death. When our physical organic cord, and the many associated cords and connections of the body cease to function, the cosmic or metaphysical cord (from which the other cords derive) asserts itself once again. This is the cord of death: that principle of connection whereby we are part of something greater than the human individuality of any one lifetime.

In some ways this is a very simple proposition, and might be summarized thus: As an individual, we are undeniably part of the natural world of planet Earth, which is undeniably part of the cosmic world of the solar system and stars. This is a physical fact that is self-evident, though there are many models of interpretation. During our lifetime, the individual (yourself), being part of a greater planetary and cosmic field, stretches its cord of connection with the natural world and the cosmos to the utmost, coming out of the vast collective into a sense of separate identity. On death, the cord of connection reasserts itself in a non-personal form. We become again part of the natural and cosmic worlds, and lose our temporary (time-bound) individuality.

The analogy is that of an elastic extension out of the greater cosmos into the manifest world of Earth and Moon, the sub-lunar world of nature. When this extension has stretched to its maximum, it starts to draw back. Eventually this elastic reflex accelerates and the life is snapped back into the metaphysical dimensions: this is the moment that we call "death".

From this place or state, of after-death and before-birth, many potentials are possible. In most cases, the individual is reborn, and so develops another biological birth and spinal cord, and lives a further life. Knowledge of the principles of the cord, however, can change this cycle. Knowledge of the Cord liberates us from the cycle of life, death, and rebirth: a liberation that extends from profound daily insights and transformations, into the greater cycles that are often regarded as immutable.

It is this knowledge that is offered in the following pages.

How to Use This Book

The Spirit Cord is in two parts: Part One is mainly exposition and exploration of concepts and practices, with some basic Cord instruction, while Part Two is mainly practical Cord exercises with additional exposition and exploration, relating to each exercise.

In Part One I have presented new insights into the found-ations of some of the most ancient and enduring sacro-magical concepts and techniques, including much that, somehow, mysteriously vanished from spiritual, magical, and occult literature of the 19th and 20th centuries, but is apt and fitting for restatement now, in the 21st. Either this material was intentionally suppressed, which I think is unlikely given the atmosphere of revelation and revolution of the 19th and early 20th century occultists, or it was simply not known to them. We can find such material in medieval and Renaissance magical philosophy and in that of the classical world and the ancient cultures if we know how to look for it. Yet it is curiously absent from modern magical and spiritual arts and practices, by which I mean those of the revival that began in the 19th century and has continued unabated through many transformations to the present day. Some of this absence is due to the appalling copyist nature of popular magical literature wherein little original work may be found. If you read very widely, you will find traces here and there, hints and obscure references. Part of my task for this book has been to present many of these ideas in a coherent form, together, in a simple text that the intelligent reader can follow ... and then go on to practice.

So I strongly encourage you to read Part One in depth before progressing to the CD and the practical work in Part Two.

There are six essential stages for ongoing work with this book and CD:

1. For maximum benefit from the text, I recommend that you read it through all the way, just as you would a novel. Do not do any of the practical work during this preliminary reading phase. Just read

it all in a relaxed manner and do not make notes. This initial reading is important, as it is in truth, the beginning of your Cord work, and lays a foundation for the more detailed practices that follow.

2. Next you should make your physical cord. Do not use a cord that you have used already for your spiritual practices, it has to be a new one: if you use a pre-existing cord (such as we are familiar with in many traditions) the result will be confusion. At a later stage, you will discover how to integrate all cords into one Cord that replaces everything else. The Cord should be of braided strands, ideally of an organic material. Thin and flexible enough to coil up and put in your pocket, or in a small bag, but strong and with some substance yet not a heavy rope. It must be as long as you are tall, no more. Some people braid their own cords or buy braided cord by the yard from a craft shop or fabric shop. The physical dimensions and material of the Cord are discussed in Part One.

3. Do nothing with your Cord yet but keep it with you, (ideally it should be wrapped comfortably around your hand), begin reading the book again, working your way in detail steadily through Part One only. At this stage you may make notes, if you must, but it is better to hold the key concepts in living memory. Later you will discover how the Cord remembers for you.

The purpose of this second reading of Part One is that the Cord, which you have not yet empowered, absorbs the content with you. Does this seem strange? Good. It is strange, for the Cord remembers everything, and from the moment you start working with it, it comes alive.

4. Now progress to Part Two. This time you do not need to read it all through unless you choose to, but you should work through the practical exercises, which are called *forms* (this use of forms is discussed later in Chapter 2).

It is essential to work through the forms steadily in order. If you jump ahead, your empowerment of the Cord will be incomplete or imbalanced. Each stage builds progressively. When we do this work with training groups, the entire cycle takes 9 months, through three weekend intensive classes and steady ongoing individual practice in between classes. If you are working from the book and CD, you can set your own pace. Regardless of how fast or slow you choose to go, work through the forms in order, every time. When you have done this cycle three times (yes, three times), you will be familiar with the material, the concepts, and the spiritual energies. Your Cord will have the primary spiritual forces woven into it, and will be attuned to the inner contacts (a theme that we will return to in the main text). Then your individual work really begins. You can subsequently work with any of the forms at any time, in any order. They all bear much fruit with regular attention and cultivation.

The order of working with the *forms* is as follows:

Basic Cord forms: chapter 6
The Crossroads: chapter 7
The Temple of Dedication: chapter 8
The Lunar Realms/The Gold and Silver Stairs: chapter 9

Chapter 6 offers direct and simple ways of working with the Cord that you can later combine with your own meditations and spiritual work. The first time around just try them out, one by one. Then move on to the essential sequence of empowerment in Chapters 7, 8, and 9. These are the three Chapters and forms that initiate, or start, the spiritual energies of the Cord and bring it alive for your ongoing work.

Once you have established and practiced this cycle of the three initiatory forms in Chapters 7, 8, and 9, at least three times, you are ready to go into deeper levels of Cord work. There are a number of other forms in the book, and now you can try those. Do not neglect the primary development forms of Crossroads, Temple, and Stairs. You should return to them often. Never fall into the modernist trap of "been there, done that, what's next?" While that attitude may suffice for trivial entertainment, magical and spiritual arts work in a very different manner. A small number of basic patterns or practices contain many levels, many possible transformations. Though the outer appearance or form remains the same, the inner content deepens, opens, and grows in power exponentially, if we stay with some simple disciplines and, most important of all, with regular practice.

5. Working with the CD. The CD that accompanies this book has all the imaginative narrative forms (empowered guided visions) that are in the book. They are uttered while working intensely with the inner visions ... they are not merely read from a script or performed. When you hear them they are happening rather than being described or dramatically presented. This is the only way in which empowered visions (visualization) can truly work from a recording. Anything else is merely a grocery list.

Each of the initiatory forms has original music, composed and recorded to assist your work with the Cord. This music comes from the inner and transformed awareness, and listening to it while in the altered state of consciousness that the forms induce, leads us into spiritual sources.

Initially, you should read through one of the key chapters (7, 8, or 9) and familiarize yourself with the contents. Work in the basic order at first, progressing through the sequence (later you can vary this according to your intention). Then, working with your Cord, listen to the CD track for your chosen chapter. Only do one of the three major and initiatory forms at a time, but you can do them in succession over three days if you wish.

When you are familiar with the three initiatory forms, and have worked with them in sequence from the CD, you are ready to successfully work with the later tracks. The later tracks are the further visionary forms in this book.

6. Working without the book and CD. The overall aim of sacro-magical Cord training, as defined in this book and CD, is to become very familiar with the forms and ultimately to participate in them in silence with complete focus and attention. Thus you should be familiar with the text first, then the recording and finally work without them. From time to time, however, I strongly recommend

that you should go back to the text, and back to the CD. Surprising developments will occur when you do this! You will discover levels within the text and responses to the recording that you were not aware of in earlier work. This occurs because we have changed as a result of our Cord work and because our Cords become increasingly empowered and attuned.

Once you have empowered your Cord, worked through the three main forms and experienced the other Cord forms and practices, your Cord will work with you and for you, in every meditation, ceremony, or aspect of sacro-magical work that you undertake. It will dream with you, remember what you think you have forgotten, and will have energizing and protective qualities. Ultimately your Cord will give you continuity and connection between many seemingly disparate aspects of your inner and outer life ... and then between more than one life.

What are we waiting for? On to Part One!

R.J. Stewart,
Vashon Island, WA
2005

Chapter 1:
CORD FORMS

1. Cord Forms and Transformation
2. Immediate Cord Magic
3. The Cord and Memory
4. Memory Reality and Conditioning
5. Memory and Experience

CORD FORMS AND TRANSFORMATION

Throughout this book, we will be working with a range of *forms*, all employing the physical cord in union with metaphysical *forces*. Forms and forces, patterns and energies. In all cases, the *form,* like a form in martial art or in dance, flows through the body. Body and Cord work together. As a result, spiritual transformations and experiences occur. The cord, be it physical or metaphysical, or a fusion of both, must never be thought of as a "symbol." It does not symbolize anything: it is a means of connection that both transcends and underpins our manifest life in the world of time, space, and interaction. We will return to this concept again in Chapter Two, but before we progress to a summary and exploration of the forms themselves, let us consider why Cord magic works, and how it works.

Immediate Cord magic

The interaction of Body and Cord works with an immediacy that is, in the modern accepted idea of magical or spiritual arts of changing consciousness/energy, unusual. But such immediacy was not unusual in older traditions of sacro-magical arts, and is, indeed, ever present and possible. The immediacy of Cord magic would not have been questioned by practitioners from most ancient times to the Renaissance. Yet 20th century consciousness limits itself, due to a complex of materialism, post-religious cultural reaction, and psychology.

Contemporary spiritual practices have been subverted, as it might be termed, by the dominance of psychology, which has become the materialist religion of the 20th century, claiming to have more or less sole ownership of knowledge and science regarding consciousness, and to offer the services of an elite priesthood of materialist therapy. Interestingly, this movement was anticipated by Rudolph Steiner long before psychology took a firm grip on modernist culture.[1]

Yet the older spiritual traditions, worldwide, all have profound and complex psychologies of their own, which reach further and delve deeper than materialism. The root of the problem is, of course, that modern psychology is the child of Judaism/Christianity and materialism, and such a curious fusion, which was a significant aspect of Western culture's emergence from 19th century rigidity, has long since passed its heyday. However, we see the influence of psychology in the work of many of the early and influential mentors of our current spiritual and magical revival. The major task of the 21st century is to go beyond this level of justification, which now seems to be somewhat naïve, though in its day it was seen as the saving tactic to make magical arts understood and respectable after a long period of opprobrium. Now we can begin to restate the magical arts in their own right, free of apologies and encumbrances.

We may explore this seeming problem by referring briefly to some concepts that are taken for granted in modern magical arts, regardless of their style, tradition, or origins. Here a few to consider:

It is often stated in books, classes, or discussions, that we must "condition" ourselves for magic to work. This is untrue. Another statement, often heard, and again seeming to stem from a (materialistic) psychological standpoint, is that we have to "believe" for something to work in magical/spiritual practices, or conversely, that lack of belief, or active disbelief, will negate magical effect. This is also untrue. Both dogmatic statements, regarding conditioning and belief, can be easily disproved by some Cord work, which shows results that have no connection to either conditioning or to belief. It is sometimes easier to "prove" practical magic to the skeptic than to the willing believer, as the skeptic has less energy invested in belief, and, expecting things not to work, is willing to be surprised and truthful when they do. The believer, however, often tries to fit his or her experience into a dogma of spiritual practice, be it Catholicism or chakra balancing.

Cord magic shows very rapidly that a direct interaction between the cord and the body will produce immediate magical transformations of consciousness and energy. In this context both conditioning and belief or disbelief are irrelevant.

The Cord and Memory

As our forebears in magic knew well, much of it depends upon memory. A great proportion of magical training was, originally, dependent upon memory, and on the properties or potentials of consciousness that had been transformed, and strengthened, by enhanced memory. When we consider, in this context, that the individual memory in our ancestral cultures was far greater than that of the present day, we seem to have our work cut out for us. The contemporary attention span has also degraded considerably, primarily as a result of generations of television watching.

Today we rely on machines for storing data ... but data is not memory, it is merely neutral content. In education we are taught to use memory in order to pass tests, but for little else. Thus our memory atrophies, especially when under pressure from media, computers, and entertainment. Little wonder that we seem to have a growing spate of attention deficiency among younger people ... they have had their inherent potential of memory stultified, and, something that is often glossed over, they are offered little that is worth paying attention to or worthy of memory. The "education" conspiracy, however, lays the blame squarely on the child, and if he or she does not enter into a docile test-passing condition, they are drugged, on the recommendation of so-called experts.

Memory is one of the prime keys to powerful magic, the other being, of course, imagination. In the average plateau levels of consciousness, day by day, if we remember something to be a certain way, then it tends to stay that way in our lives unless a significant force of change realigns it. This is true for the individual, and especially true for the collective. Much of the so-called present is based upon structures of memory of the so-called past. The memory that we cite here is what might be called the surface of memory, that which is most easily accessible as, in many cases, a false or delusional check list of "that which is known." This quality of memory imprinting derives from something that we discuss in Chapter 4, the metaphysical teaching regarding imprints of the astral light, or stellar consciousness. At this stage, however, we do not need this teaching to follow the discussion on functions of memory within either day by day consciousness and habit, or in magical arts and cord work.

There are several powerful spiritual techniques which consist of letting go of the false check list, and seeking to un-know. This is not, however, the same as forgetting, and in practice such techniques of "unknowing" greatly enhance our living creative memory, and therefore expand consciousness. Furthermore, the expansion of consciousness that occurs as a result of such specific (and unusual) changes in the memory, is far greater than modern individuals might expect, and brings many surprises.

Memory, Reality, and Conditioning

The idea that memory is the key to transforming individual and consensual reality is a very different proposition to that of psychological conditioning, though it seems likely that the concept and practice of conditioning, as defined in the various schools of psychology, arises from a limited understanding of this vital property of memory.

The use of memory in magical and spiritual work deserves further exploration, and in this context of the sacred Cord and consciousness, we can go some way towards defining how memory works in spiritual and magical arts.

Memory and Experience

On a simple day-by-day, year-by-year basis, most of what we experience is forgotten, in favor of a memory plateau or false check list of that which is known, that which makes the identity. Overall this leads to the idea that we live a linear life ... of course we do, because we believe that we can *remember* its progression from childhood to the present! Yet the perennial spiritual traditions advise us that we live many other lives simultaneously, or have been within other lives in other time-frames, and that we have many experiences other than those of the consensual outer world or limited personal emotional world. All of these are, usually, forgotten. If other memories intrude on the limited checklist, they are usually distressing, uncomfortable, or regarded as signs of "mental illness" or "disorder." The very fact that memories outside the highly suppressive framework of post-Christian modernist culture are said to be undesirable, even dangerous, should give us a hint as to how significant memory really is in our establishing of both an individual and consensual reality. This modernist culture seeks, virulently and ceaselessly, to limit and imprison awareness, through drugs/medication and through media of entertainment and so-called communication. If your awareness does not confirm, drug it. If you are still unhappy, escape through watching television, communicate only through digital interfaces, with as little human interaction as possible. Feelings become emoticons, memory is deadened by chemicals, awareness withers.

As is often said, our low ebb of consciousness, our forgetting is usually a good thing: contrary to our assumptions and self-image, the temporal or outer personality is held together by forgetting, rather than by remembering! The personality forgets especially anything that might jeopardize its self-image or entity. In a highly pressurized and dehumanized modernist culture, forgetting is one of the cruder and more effective ways of relating and coping. Assisted by drugs and television, it works shockingly well, as millions will attest. Eventually the personality lives vicariously through entertainment, and the "life-style" of highly manipulated consumer groups. At its worst, the personality becomes voyeuristic, an increasing trait created by, and fed by, television entertainment. In Chapter 5 we explore some of the essential guidelines for freedom from the suppressive forces of modernist culture, especially in the context of the imagination. We are so imbued with our media, that we tend to forget that if the plug were pulled, it would all cease in an instant ... a delusion evaporated. A slight change in our star, our sun, may stop our electricity at any time, as the influence of sunspots on modern technology amply demonstrates.

So the human being easily forgets, and often this is good. The memory that cleanses and disposes is part of the eliminatory system, and not to be feared or fought. But our awareness of this forgetting creates a counter-movement in which we keep our linear checklist of our "self." Some people find this check list in attainment, in promotion, in the family, in their looks, in their sexuality, in a thousand other ways. But it is only a trick of memory, an illusion of temporal continuity and self-justification. We forget our spiritual nature, our other consciousness, our reaching out to the thresholds of awareness. Indeed, much of the medication and entertainment cycle, the endless loop of mind-death, is intentionally designed and implemented to limit severely such movement.

The Cord, however, forgets nothing. Its metaphysical nature, as an embodiment of *that which connects*, is inherent and active in its physical substance. Your physical Cord remembers everything that happens, stores it, and can recall it when in contact with your body. If that which is stored in the Cord is a series of spiritual experiences and a focused conflation of spiritual contacts, then this is what the Cord can, and does translate instantly back into the body. Our Cord forms throughout this book are intended to create and establish exactly such a series of experiences and such a focusing of interlaced inner contacts. All of the foregoing is present in the substance of the Cord, and ultimately accessible through touch. Put the Cord on or lay it out, and something happens. Take it off and put it away, and the subtle energies reduce their flow, though in truth they never stop once your Cord has been progressively empowered and contacted.

We will return to the subject of *inner contacts* in several places as we progress, for without them, most magic fails. This essential work with inner or spiritual contacts is the mirror image of the human outer life, wherein most endeavors will fail without human contact. For the inner life and inner community we need inner or spirit contacts: for the outer we need fellow humans. The Cord connects to a transpersonal memory field, which encompasses all such contacts, and much more, beyond time. Yet practical Cord work brings these spiritual forces of memory back into the body, into the mind/brain interaction, and from there, into our surface consciousness.

This transpersonal memory is why Cord magic seems instantaneous, for, although the day by day personality forgets the spiritual experiences, often immediately after having them (a well known situation for meditators), the Cord reconnects the memories through the body.

This interaction alters that plateau of memory within time and space, wherein we live through habit and consensus, that mode of filtered and severely limited memory that creates the illusion of the linear life. The Cord enables us to move both above and below the plateau of memory, free of even the most outwardly-directed awareness. These OverWorld and UnderWorld levels are what are usually termed the metaphysical realms, though they have their physical embodiments in the planetary depths, the UnderWorld, and the Solar System and Stars, the OverWorld. We should consider that the physical world is held together by memory also, a memory that is present in shapes, in entities, and in interactions. Our human memory partakes in this vast collective memory of the world, but is not necessarily bound by it.

With practice, the inherent quality of connection, embodied in the Cord, will lead to deep and transcendent experiences. These include transformation of memory, new modes of memory, and the much discussed seldom experienced memories of "other lives," a subject that we will explore further in our later chapters.

Note(s)

1. *Psychoanalysis and Spiritual Psychology, 5 lectures,* Rudolf Steiner, Introduction by Robert Sardello, Steiner Books, Anthroposophic Press, August 1990.

Chapter 2:
THE CORD OF CONNECTION

1. Our Connection Between Lives
2. Popular Notions of Past Lives, Unity, Individuality
3. All is One?
4. The Cord is Not a Symbol
5. Memory of Past Lives
6. Dissolving the Delusion of Time
7. Three Aspects of Cord Work
8. Why Connect?

OUR CONNECTION BETWEEN LIVES

The cord is that which *connects*; between spatial physical locations, metaphysical locations, individuals, entities, and discrete consciousness interacting within a sequence of time. Just as our modern science tells us that minute connectors in the nervous system keep us together as an entity physically, so does metaphysics and sacromagical art offer us insights into other aspects of connection, equally subtle, but not limited to the physical body, and not terminated at physical death. Indeed, physical death opens us to connections that were dulled or obscure during our manifest lives, just as physical birth re-establishes our connections with the world of nature. Such connections may be understood, and worked with, on three levels: the microcosmic which is within the human body and consciousness, the macrocosmic, which is throughout the universe, and a third or median level, which interleaves with both. This third mode of connection is of especial interest and practical significance in cord magic, and comes into effect when we work with the astral double of our cords (see Chapter Four).

Essential for us in our practical work is this concept: the cord connects between lives, the lives of individual entities, from microbes to stars, and the many lives of any one entity. For you, as a human on planet Earth, *the cord is that factor of continuity which connects your many lives as one*. These many lives come into and exit from manifestation in nature, but they are all "you." Just as piece of string connects two locations, one at each end, and will scribe a circle if one end is fixed and the other is free. This quality or concept of "cordness" or "stringness" is what we work with in our conscious spiritual disciplines regarding continuity between lives. The outer cord is a piece of rope, the inner cord is that quality and *property of connection* that is exhibited in the outer world by the way in which a physical rope or string can and does move, connect, shape, and contain or liberate any set of points, locations, entities, that would seem to be otherwise unconnected and "separate." The Cord creates, defines, and modulates connections. It obviates isolation, but also selects and shapes patterns of connection, moving always towards harmony, working through whatever is needful, apt, and fitting for individual transformation. More simply, we can assert that an empowered Cord tunes our connections to all things, selectively, protectively, creatively.

POPULAR NOTIONS OF PAST LIVES, UNITY, AND INDIVIDUALITY

At this point in the exposition, we should be cautious about two popular ideas that are very widespread as a result of the contemporary spiritual revival. They are the idea that "all is one," and the idea of recovery of "memory" of past lives. Both have deep pitfalls in their presentation as popularly circulated and accepted. Like many popularized spiritual themes at this time, they appear to offer liberating ideas, but can lead to severe restriction through delusion and ego-inflation.

ALL IS ONE?

All is One? It has become fashionable, even standard, to accept without deep thought, and to repeatedly assert, that "all is one." While such words are fine, and truly inspiring, the mental concept, the words alone, are often misleading, especially in a world where it is obvious that all is not one, a world of conflict, inequity, and oppression. To simply assert that all is one, or I am the cosmos, or all is bliss, may lead to escapism or ego-inflation. To sense feel and know that all is one, implies that we must also pass through much suffering and pain, for those others who suffer are also One. It is not surprising that the superficial All-Is-Oner either drops out at this stage, or retreats into an egocentric fantasy world (all-is-one, I-create-my-own-reality), refusing responsibility or participation. It is for this very reason that the best teachings of both Buddhism and Christianity emphasize, in their different ways, that spiritual transformation cannot occur without compassion. The same concept is found in mystical Islam and in the various traditions of Qabalah. In all such examples compassion is not a feeling ... it is not sentiment. Compassion is a spiritual force, and must be experienced in a deep and irrevocable manner. Little wonder then, that many people prefer a comfortable delusion of spirituality to a demanding spiritual reality.

This apparent dilemma and delusion over the grandiose idea of all-is-one should not arise in our practices with the cord. If it does arise, the cord practices will disassemble it, unravel its egocentric knot, and connect the psychic energies thus liberated to a deeper level of consciousness.

The qualities of connection that we are emphasizing in cord magic do, indeed, come from the universal unity of Being. The cord, however, is not That; but it is, subtly, *whatever connects the many aspects of That,* of Universal Being through time, space, and movement. Thus it is both (1) a philosophical concept of connection, and (2) any practical form that connects, manifests and exhibits that philosophical concept in action. It is also, most significant for us as humans on Earth, a third thing: a physical cord ... be it of silk, hemp, straw, skin and blood or nerve tissue.

All Being is One, but the cord enables us to discover the mysterious strands of connection between apparently separate aspects of that Being. The *apparent separation* is through time, space, and movement; the *inherent continuity* is through timeless connection ... embodied for us, in this spiritual art, by the cord. Apparent separation and inherent continuity are mutually interlaced, and this concept is of considerable benefit to us in meditation. This theme is beautifully expressed in the prose poem *Orchil*, by the 19th century mystic Fiona Macleod/William Sharp, which is quoted in Appendix Two with a short commentary.

THE CORD IS NOT A SYMBOL

Always remember that the cord is not symbolic. The physical cord that you work with does not symbolize anything ... if you think of it as such, it will have little power. The popularization of symbols (no doubt due to the wide acceptance of psychology) has greatly enervated magical practice. Instead of accepting something as it is, and working with it, relating to it, we tend to ask "what does it symbolize?" Of course many aspects of magic involve symbolism, but we have somehow forgotten that many do not. A lion may indeed symbolize strength, but it is also a lion. A lion mediates, directly as a living creature, many spiritual powers. It is not a symbol.

The tendency to move all magical or spiritual embodiments into an intellectual abstraction of themselves, into simulacra devolved from their originals, is one of the greatest deceits of modernist culture[1].

The cord connects through all worlds; therefore your physical cord connects to other aspects of the cord in metaphysical dimensions. That is why a physical cord is so important for us while we are working in this world ... and why the astral cord, which is discussed in Chapter 4, is so important for us in that mysterious realm between lives, between death and rebirth. This theme of death and rebirth brings us to the second of the popular pitfalls mentioned above.

MEMORY OF PAST LIVES?

Do we have true memory of past lives? One of the hidden spiritual arts is that of maintaining continuity between lives. The cord assists us with such continuity, for it exists independently of time. Thus we can connect to our spiritual cord repeatedly through many lifetimes, no matter what we forget during the death and rebirth processes.

At this level of connection, the cord is not a means of linear memory. The usual interpretation of so-called "memory of past lives" seems to involve a linear memory ... I was this, I did that, I remember being such. Yet this approach, which is bound by the delusion of linear time, is extremely super-ficial, as the true life is the inner or spiritual life, not the details of the outer. This is so important for us, that it is worth expanding somewhat and repeating:

The true life is the inner or spiritual life, not the details of the outer story or personal drama. Thus attempting to remember the details of a past life as linear events, and as substituted explanations for, or confirmations of, or inter-pretations (or excuses) concerning the present life problems, is a dangerous delusion that severely limits spiritual development.

The popular idea of seeming to remember traumatic experiences from previous lives, often generated through hypnosis, is sought as a fatuous explanation of problems in the present, yet falls far short of our inherent capability to connect between lives. And, once again, it can lead to an artificial inflation of the ego. My favorite naïve example of such inflation was a gentleman who said to me, with great seriousness: "I cannot tell you who I was in my past life, as it is a secret. But beginning next month I am going to study carpentry." I would have been more impressed if he had said that he had started carpentry immediately … beginning next month is too late.

Dissolving the Delusion of Time

There are several ways of dissolving the consensual delusion of linear time. The most simple is to throw away all your phones, cell phones, computers watches and clocks: remove every mechanical or electronic time-measuring device from your life. But that is absolutely not allowed in the modernist world: we are slaves of time, especially of that binding time that is asserted and imposed upon us by others. One way towards liberation from temporal delusion is to consider this: all lives are present lives. For example, you never think "hmm…I am in a past life right now." All lives are present lives. We live all of our lives in the present, and nowhere else. Meditate on this, and it will free you from the consensual delusion of time.

The cord provides not only connection, but direct practical means whereby we may recover and maintain our awareness of continuity. Thus we can discover, and participate within, our long-term life patterns, those deep patterns that emit many lives, and are of greater significance to us than any single life story. Ultimately the cord brings us into a conscious awareness of our inner Being, of that which connects all to All.

This is a very different process to verbally declaring all-is-one and trying to remember the petty details of so-called past lives.

While we have no historical or archaeological or textual proof, I am certain that this sacromagical art of the cord formed one of the deepest inner trainings of the priest and priestesshood of the ancestral temples, be they temples of stone, or of trees, of the volcano, or of the island, the desert, or the ocean shore.

THREE ASPECTS OF CORD WORK

There are three interconnected aspects of cord work, and these are presented in this book: one third proportion of what is offered comes from our inner contacts, those transhuman mentors within the Inner Convocation of the Inner Temples, while another third is comes through accessing memory of cord arts through time, and the last and deepest third part comes directly from working with the cord itself. All three are open to you through the methods offered here.

WHY CONNECT?

It might be argued that we are avoiding one of the most basic questions in this exposition: why connect at all? Do we really need to consciously connect across multiple lives? The simple answer is no, we do not. The multiple lives are inherently connected, regardless of our awareness, interest, disinterest, or delusion. The key concept in all magical or spiritual work is that of *conscious participation*. If you wish to consciously participate in a life greater than the individual petty drama, cord magic is one such method.

A human being lives many lives. The manifestation of these lives is not linear, as is often supposed, but like a loose network or web, portions of which dip in and out of the sea of consensual time. When we are within that sea (of collective consciousness of humanity) we are aware only of those strands of the net that are dipped, and our present life is upon a node of one such strand. When we move out of the collective consciousness, we become more aware of the web, of the pattern, most of which is, so to speak, above water. When we come into an expanded awareness of connection, we eventually discover that the web enfolds the entire sphere of time/space/interaction. What we used to think of as moving upwards or *out* of the delusion of time, becomes a movement towards a consciousness that *enfolds* time.

This pattern of the web of greater awareness enfolding time is mirrored in the weaving of the sphere of the sub-lunar world ... that web woven around our planet earth by the orbit of the Moon.

Meditations upon this network or web are extremely productive: while doing so, your physical cord should be used according the Cord Forms described in Chapter 5.

This brings us to a key concept for transformation and for effective work in all conscious magic, that of the *evolutionary and involutionary streams*. Before we can use our Cords effectively, we must discover how these twin streams flow, and how to flow with them.

Note(s)

1. *Simulacra and Simulation,* J. Baudrillard, trans. by Sheila Faria Glaser, University of Michigan Press, 1994

CHAPTER 3:
THE TWIN STREAMS

1. The Evolutionary and Involutionary Streams
2. The Two Streams and Involution/Evolution
3. The Theft of Meaning
4. Defining Evolution
5. The Evolution of Modern Culture
6. Defining Involution
7. Wrapping and Rolling, In and Out
8. The Origins of the Streams

THE EVOLUTIONARY AND INVOLUTIONARY STREAMS

In this chapter we explore the concepts and teachings regarding the involutionary and evolutionary streams that flow into and out of our planet, circulating within the cosmos. The physical manifestations of these streams, such as the various radiations emitted and received by the stars and planets, are studied by our contemporary sciences. Their metaphysical forces have long been described in the perennial spiritual and magical traditions, and these subtle forces affect life and consciousness just as much as the measured radiations of the sun and stars, or the geomagnetic forces of Moon and Earth. Indeed, both the physical and metaphysical effects of the streams are aspects of the same cosmic circulation and relative polarities of energy.

Traditionally these polarised forces, incoming and outgoing, on-planet and off-planet, have long been described as *streams*. We will stay with this traditional convention, as there are many visions, sources, and concepts that are greatly enabled thereby. In modern cosmology, we may conceive of the total body of the Earth radiating forces outwards. This is, effectively, a "spherical" field of outward radiation, though its shape changes and is constantly in flux. We may also conceive of the myriad forces of the solar system and cosmos, reaching to the Earth, reaching the planet from all around, effectively as a sphere of inward radiation. Such spheres or polarities of outgoing and incoming energies are well described by physics.

The two streams of the esoteric metaphysical traditions are exactly the same forces, of the Earth and of the cosmos, but in modes of energy and consciousness that are not described in a physical model. Nowadays, we often hear that quantum physics provides models that are similar to those of magic and metaphysics. In these models the consciousness affects the possible outcome of any situation. I am not fully convinced by such arguments. They are similar to the justifications of magic via psychology that were offered in the early 20th centuries. There is no more need to justify the perennial wisdom traditions by quantum physics than there is to justify them by materialist psychology. But, at least, quantum physics seems to describe a universe that is similar to that perceived in spiritual contemplation and long described in the sacro-magical traditions – a world in which consciousness affects the outcome of events.

In the vast exchange of cosmic energies the two streams referred to in the spiritual traditions (that radiate out of and into our planet Earth) are in effect, known to us whenever we focus on the polarity of the exchange. In other words, they are not the entire field of forces as that is too vast for us to comprehend except in the abstract. They are segments or bands of the incoming/outgoing exchange. These are two streams or flows, intentionally defined from out of the vast interchange between Earth, the Solar System, and the cosmos. These flows are identifiable and can be worked with just as we may identify and work with the ocean currents, or the tide paths and currents of a bay, river, or stream.

The flow of the two streams, into and out of our world, our bodies, and our awareness, has a powerful, inevitable, effect upon us, and may be utilised consciously in our sacromagical work. Cord *forms* place emphasis upon working intentionally with streams. In Appendix 3, you will find an essay on the streams as they are described in ancient sources, in the Faery and UnderWorld traditions. In these sources they appear as red and white dragons, and underground rivers of blood and tears that circulate within the earth. The idea of the twin or polarised streams has been described for centuries in ancestral traditions and is found deep within religion, magic, mysticism, and philosophy. In our present context, we are exploring it afresh, discovering applications for our Cord forms.

THE TWO STREAMS AND INVOLUTION/EVOLUTION

As an essential foundation for our practical work, we should explore the deeper meaning of the terms evolution and involution. Our exploration begins with a short discussion of the loss of meaning in modernist media culture. This loss, and warping, of meaning of words and concepts, is deeply magical and extremely pernicious. Anyone engaged in magical or spiritual work must become acutely aware of the distortion of words and concepts that is, for most people, the mental and psychic field in which we live. For the practical magician, this distortion changes many of the older methods of magic, and is extremely suppressive.

THE THEFT OF MEANING

We live in a time when many meanings, ideas, concepts and hallowed images are taken and twisted into parodies of themselves for manipulative purposes. Obvious examples abound in advertising and politics that affect us and often gain responses, even when we know that they are lies. Yet these are merely the scum on the top of a thick soup of perverted meaning in our culture. Such widespread theft of meaning is not as superficial as we might think, for the roots of words reach into the roots of consciousness itself. In an age when everyone seems to own trivialised and popularised instant pseudo-knowledge of so much, resulting in surprisingly little, it is easy to manipulate meaning, consciousness and imagery.

If we are involved in spiritual work, relating directly with living consciousness, we should first thoughtfully explore the meaning of some of the key terms that we use. This exploration is, in itself, a magical and spiritual act of considerable power. To work effectively with the evolutionary and involutionary streams of consciousness and cosmic energy, we must first understand the words that we use to describe them. We must also strip from those words the accumulated trivia and dualism of our modernist popularised knowledge. It is important to not forget to be ruthless with those vague terms inherent in our own spiritual revival in its many variants. Only then can we proceed to pass with power into the deeper realms of awareness.

Defining Evolution

The term "evolution" is often found in the literature and teachings of our current spiritual revival. It is one of those terms that everyone understands, or so it would seem. Evolution is frequently quoted for a variety of purposes and with a wide range of definitions. The ideal of spiritual evolution is loosely applied to any concept of transformation or self-development, often with an emphasis upon the *self*, or individual. However, there are differing modes and levels of "self." The contemporary emphasis upon self-development tends, regrettably, albeit innocently, to have an egocentric flare. The true self is not the temporally bound and evanescent personality, but a deeper self that both transcends and founds many lives and personae. Through our sacromagical Cord work we can discover our true nature, our non-personal self.

When we contemplate the deeper implications of evolution and involution in terms of "self" the customary self identification, that of the personality, soon fades into insignificance. As this can be a somewhat disturbing process, at least in its initial stages, we should begin by building a strong foundation upon which to rest. The mental/intellectual substance of this foundation comprises a clear understanding of the inner, spiritual, or esoteric teachings on evolution and involution.

Let us begin with some definitions and explorations of the concept of Evolution. A typical dictionary search shows the following five definitions, or close variants.

1. Evolution: A gradual process in which something changes into a different and usually more complex form.

2. In *Biology:* Change in the genetic composition of a population during successive generations, as a result of natural selection acting on the genetic variation among individuals, and resulting in the development of new species.

3. A movement that is part of a set of ordered movements.

4. In *mathematics*: The extraction of a root of a quantity.

5. A continuing process of change from one state or condition to another or from one form to another.

When we look into the origins of a word, we also touch upon its roots in consciousness and ancestral memory. The word that we use today comes from Latin, from *voltus*, past participle of *volvere*, to unroll. To evolve is to e-volve, to roll out.

All of the foregoing actions of evolution require movement, or rolling. They describe movement away from an existing form or condition, towards another form or condition.

The Evolution of Modern Culture

There is a desperate emotionally laden tendency in contemporary thought for "evolution" to equate with "better." We will return to this notion again, as it is fraught with illusion and immature dualistic rejection. It derives from a widespread, almost dogmatised, general trivialising and misconception of the Darwinian thesis. It becomes a creed in which old is bad and new is good ... let's escape from whatever we do not like into something better; usually taking no responsibility for cleaning up behind us. New products are better than old - technology evolves at a rapid rate. We have all heard this shrill dogma many times. Such ideas are clearly absurd when we consider them in this satirical manner, yet they are at the very foundation of much of modernist culture. We take them for granted every day in thousands of ways.

If we pause for a moment to consider what really happens, we find that modern technology does not truly evolve. It develops in a highly eccentric yet planned manner according to commercial manipulation. In some examples it remains static, while in others it leaps ahead wherever profit is sniffed out. Many fine developments in science, especially practical applications that might improve life, destroy less of the environment and compassionately benefit the needy are intentionally suppressed or banned. Such a process whereby beneficial advances are wilfully discounted and disallowed cannot be called evolution - except perhaps in the distorted realm of the advertising copywriter or the politician.

If science was actively supported in our culture, which in truth it is not, and was allowed to evolve freely, the scientific utopian dream of our forebears would truly begin to arise from its uneasy slumber. Today, in the 21st century, we know that this utopian scientific dream of the 18th and 19th centuries is an illusion, and furthermore, we know that it cannot, and will not, be allowed by vested interests.

So it might be superficially thought that the manipulation of technology for commercial and political ends may equate to involution, rather than evolution. Yet, if we accept this, we accept the trivialisation of meaning for both evolution and involution as valuable concepts. When we examine the root meaning of involution, we will find something very different indeed from suppression and manipulation – or failure to evolve.

Evolution cannot exist without involution, and we must somehow learn how to value both equally, as we live within the tides of both on all levels of our being.

Let us now consider the meaning of involution:

DEFINING INVOLUTION

A typical dictionary search will find the following five definitions, or close variants.

1. Involution: the act of involving. The state of being involved.

2. Intricacy; complexity.

3. *In Mathematics:* An operation, such as negation, which, when applied to itself, returns the original number.

4. *In Embryology:* The in-growth and curling inward of a group of cells, as in the formation of a gastrula from a blastula.

5. *In Medicine:* A decrease in size of an organ, as of the uterus following childbirth. A progressive decline or degeneration of normal physiological functioning occurring as a result of the aging process.

The Latin source for our modern word is involutus, past participle of involvere, *to enwrap.* Once again, remember that the origins of a word in contemporary language point to its origins in consciousness and ancestral memory. Thus exploration of a Latin source is far more than an academic footnote in a dictionary. The development of words through time reveals a flow of *consciousness,* a woven cord-of-meaning. For this reason we must be extremely cautious when words with deep and enduring meanings are hijacked, intentionally, in modern usage and propaganda.

From an inner perspective, such hijacking creates a knot in the cord-of-meaning, or even misdirects it entirely. The seizure and appropriation of a word, especially a word with deep concepts and spiritual implications, is a magical act of theft – a theft of power. Power is taken from us all when such a theft occurs.

WRAPPING AND ROLLING, IN AND OUT

From the dictionary definitions and Latin roots, we discover that to *evolve* is to roll out or unwrap, and to *involve* is to enwrap or roll in. Both require movement, and both cause a change from an existing form or condition into a new form or condition. The difference is one of *direction*. Note carefully that the direction taken creates either a wrapping (involution) or an unwrapping (evolution). This is vitally important in our spiritual context and central to our cord work.

By approaching the concepts of evolution and involution in this manner, we can begin to do away with dualism or emotive value based use of these words. Use of the word evolution is loaded with emotional dualism and false values especially in the New Age spiritual revival where it often implies ego-inflation and irresponsible escapism. Yet those who use the word in this manner are actually using it in a materialistic sense. For example, evolution popularly implies a self-development, the bigger-better-faster urge of modernism, such as the "evolution of technology," which is really the expansion and ephemeralism of commercial products for profit, be they soap, soup, or military missiles. A similar notion of modernism, of bigger-and-better is also declared to be happening within the soul, the psyche and the spirit. It is the growth of the New Age that is, so we are told, visible and evident all around us. Presumably this evidence is visible if we choose to ignore little things such as pandemic disease, starvation and suffering, terrorism, human exploitation, ongoing deforestation and the overall collapse of planetary economy. Provided we do not even think about these, the New Age is already upon us, and we are spiritually evolved!

Yet, if you have done more than three minutes of meditation, it is clear that this application of the highly manipulative concepts of modernistic development is invalid in the spiritual realms. It is, in short, a delusion. It is not so much a case that, as in the old parable, the emperor is wearing no clothes but that he is all clothes and there is no emperor within.

The concept of the Evolutionary and Involutionary streams, or movements, is found in many books and teachings, and is central to the writing of esotericists such as Rudolph Steiner, and later, Dion Fortune. Both are highly influential thinkers and proponents of spiritual tradition, albeit in different ways. It is this esoteric or inner meaning, upheld by perennial spiritual tradition and teaching, that we need for our cord work. It may be summarized as follows:

1. Involutionary movement is that which moves on-planet: from the Stars, through the Solar system, to the world of Earth and Moon.

2. Evolutionary movement is that which moves off-planet: from the world of Earth and Moon, to the Solar system, to the Stars.

This is clearly shown in physics by the radiant energies that are both emitted and received by our planet Earth and our Moon, exchanging with both the solar system and the cosmos. In the metaphysical realms, the flow and exchange continues through many dimensions, and this is what concerns us in our spiritual work with the Cord.

With involution we become enwrapped in the sub-lunar and earth world. With evolution we unfold those wrappings and move away. These are the sheaths or robes so often referred to in esoteric and magical teachings. They lead during involution to the physical body – to birth – to manifestation. Death, therefore, is part of our evolution. We will return to this concept often and specifically when we discuss the Cord of Life and Death in detail. The main problem that we have with this remarkable perennial teaching is that it has become propagandized and rendered dualistic and antagonistic. Involution is supposedly bad and evolution is good, so we are told. But we are further conflicted because we also think that death, essentially a potent evolutionary change, is bad ... we want to live forever, of course, and often claim that we want to *evolve* as humans. By which we often mean that we do not want to change, merely to become more selfishly immobile and unassailable by surprise. So how can we come into a more balanced understanding?

The Origins of the Streams

Thus far we have merely clarified definitions and reasserted something that is widely agreed in spiritual and magical circles: evolution leads off-planet, involution leads on-planet. But we have intentionally avoided in our definitions to use terms like "higher" and "lower" levels, planes, or orders of being. These are all the result of pernicious dualism, and must be regarded as tools of suppression and ignorance, no matter how rarified their presentation.

Where is above? It is an illusion created by gravity. The Stars are not above us, they have never been, and never will be. They are all around us.

Where is below? Is below relatively inferior in quality to above? Not so, for Below is in the center of the earth, the center of a sphere of consciousness. It might be argued that Below, the Center of our planet, in terms of relativity, is the center of universe. Below, as centrality, derives from Place and Observation. Where you are *is* the center. You are the Earth as you read this.

Let us consider cosmic origins as defined in our perennial spiritual traditions worldwide. Origins arising from our deepest intuitions and roots of consciousness, wherein *nothing* becomes *something* through a mysterious movement. This teaching seems to be mirrored today in many popular presentations of contemporary physics and quantum theory.

The Streams originate at the very core and first movement of the cosmos, of Becoming out of the Void. One flows Out, the other flows In.

In Qabalistic mysticism and cosmology, the Streams are defined by the 2nd and 3rd emanations or spheres of the Tree of Life, often termed Wisdom and Understanding, the Star Father, the Deep Mother, Out-reaching, In-drawing. But we should ask which is which ... which is *evolutionary* and which is *involutionary*?

This is what a lawyer would call a vexatious question, especially as it has no fixed and firm answer and may never be judged in this world. The *evolutionary* stream or movement from the Void outwards towards manifestation is also, further along its movement, its cosmic flow, the *involutionary* stream bringing us into form and flesh on Earth. The *involutionary* stream or movement back into the Void is, from an Earth based perspective, the *evolutionary* stream that carries us away from form and flesh into stars and spirit.

Thus, for us, the polarity of the streams is reversed, and changes according to our perspective. If we are unaware of the streams, we are passively subject to them. Birth and death are aspects of our long cycle of many involutions and evolutions. If we are aware of the streams, and participate in them intentionally, we discover how to work the reversed polarities. We will return to this concept again.

As far as we, and all beings on Earth, are concerned the involutionary stream that has an undeniable influence upon us is that tidal force of the sub-lunar world. It brings us into biological form and sways the rhythm of our consciousness and energy from before birth until after death. The evolutionary stream is that other power which dissolves form and causes our awareness to change direction at the time of death. Thus, in the most direct sense, birth is involutionary and death is evolutionary.

In our next chapter we explore how the Cord may exist beyond time between death and rebirth. As part of that exploration we reclaim certain key terms in magical and spiritual arts and disciplines, terms that have become corrupted and confused in modern publication and popular use.

CHAPTER 4:
THE ASTRAL DOUBLE OF THE CORD

1. The Astral Double of the Cord
2. Redefining Some Terminology
3. The Astral Plane and the Sub-Lunar World
4. Differences Between Material Psychology and Esoteric Psychology
5. What is the Astral Double?
6. Countless Astral Doubles
7. Further Definition of the Astral Double
8. Types of Astral Double
9. Archetypes and Astral Doubles
10. Imprinting the Astral Light
11. Creating and Maintaining the Cord Double

THE ASTRAL DOUBLE OF THE CORD

We now come to a major practice of cord magic. It is a practice that is almost unknown in modern literature, because the method has not been taught in the popular magical/spiritual revival which began in the mid-19th century and which continues in many presentations to this day. This major practice, or spiritual art, involves the *astral double* of the cord which develops through two stages. The first stage is establishing an astral double, and the second is working with it long term. Indeed, the long term work extends over many lifetimes, a concept that we will revisit in various parts of this book and that we started to explore in Chapter Two: *Connection between Lives*.

REDEFINING SOME TERMINOLOGY

Before we proceed to the forms for this aspect of cord work, we should establish, and indeed reclaim, a working definition of the "astral double." Due to 19th century occultism and, especially, to copyist tendencies in later popular literature, the terms *astral* and *astral double* have become severely debased currency. These misconceptions have appeared because of ignorance and misuse in fiction and in New Age or spiritualistic/channeling literature. Today, the popular idea of the term astral is different from its original, true and spiritually valuable meaning.

A classic example of this debasement process is found in the popular phrase "the astral plane" when it is used to describe a psychic energetic zone only a step or two away from the manifest world. This "astral plane," in truth, is the realm of hungry ghosts, phantoms, and desire-driven thought-forms. It is a place, or no-place, which sometimes acts as a temporary dwelling for those who have recently died, especially if intense desire, habituated sexual fantasy, strong emotion, pain or violence attended the death. This "astral plane," despite all the many cautions offered in literature, is also said to be the medium or menstruum for "astral travel." There is a repetitive heap of popular books describing how we might come out of our bodies and fly free "on the astral."

This astral plane, or zone of consciousness and energy, is also encountered during certain kinds of dreaming. Most modern readers are familiar with this somewhat lurid dogma, even if it is only through fiction. Anyone who has tried to test the popularly published methods of "astral travel" will confirm, if they are truthful, that such methods do not work. This is because they have never worked for anyone, rather than through any failing on our part to understand or to practice the methods.

One of the curious traps found in both New Age dogma and commercial occultism is that is when a much-touted method fails to work, the student is told that he or she is "not ready." With practical analysis, we eventually discover that some methods simply do not work, no matter how ready we may be!

If one dares to challenge the published teachings on "astral travel," or the monolithic central New Age dogma of "chakras" (another much misrepresented teaching) the challenge leads to extreme shock and/or a violent reaction from readers or listeners. Sadly there is as much dogma in occultism and in the New Age movement as can be found at a fundamentalist convention or a papal conclave.

As an aside, it should be affirmed that effective distance contact, or distance traveling (visual or mental/telepathic) does not require so-called astral travel, and that there are many ways of enabling this type of travel that can be found in the spiritual and magical traditions worldwide. We will explore some of these, as cord forms, in our later chapters. You can find many such distance contact methods preserved in folkloric traditions: some are co-operative, some coercive.

Returning to the idea of astral travel and the astral plane, we can be generous to a certain extent and say that, in a very broad sense, *all* of the popular propaganda on "the astral" is somewhat accurate, albeit greatly confused by copyists. Some of the methods described *may* be possible to achieve although, there are much easier methods that work with greater clarity and substantially less risk. But here is the crucial truth: *the popular teaching on the subject does not describe or involve the true astral plane*. It refers instead, ignorantly in most cases, to a realm more earthy, that realm which permeates the zone between Moon and Earth. The old medieval magicians, drawing upon classical and native sources, and the Renaissance magicians of the 15th and 16th centuries, knew exactly what this realm is, and they defined working within it in detail. They called it the *sub-lunar world*. A world of consciousness and energy that is just behind, beyond and before, the manifest world.

The *astral* plane, however, is exactly what its name states: the realm of the stars. Astral means Starry. It has always meant Starry ... it does not mean psychic or sub-lunar or dream world or anything else that is often called "astral" in popular literature.

Differences Between Material Psychology and Esoteric Psychology

There is another misleading idea, often published and mis-taught, that the astral plane is an earlier occult definition of the unconscious or subconscious mind. Such ideas began to creep into esoteric and magical books in the 20th century, when occultists tried, unsuccessfully and unnecessarily, to gain respectability and justification by drawing comparisons between occultism magic and psychology. This identification of the "astral" plane with the subconscious or unconscious is but one aspect of the subtle, or sometimes gross, misappropriation of spiritual and magical terms from the ancient traditions by materialist psychology.

Such identification of the astral plane and the subconscious realms, as is sometimes proposed by materialist psychology, is not accurate or valid. Nor has the sub-lunar world of traditional magic ever been the unconscious mind, even when it is called the "astral plane" through copyist ignorance. There are areas and images of the unconscious mind, both individual and collective, which most certainly resonate with forces in the sub-lunar world. They are not limited to, or contained within, the individual human mind. *The mind does not contain the cosmos nor any part of it, for the cosmos contains the mind.* Thus the cosmos is all Mind, but not the self-referring human mind. This is the significant difference between a materialist psychology and an esoteric psychology.

The Astral Plane and the Sub-Lunar World

If we were to talk with Dr. John Dee, or Giordiano Bruno, they would tell us exactly what the astral plane is. It is the Star world:

the realm of matrices and potentials for all being. It is that realm that has its physical manifestation in nebulae, clouds of stars, and galaxies, and has its spiritual source in the Universal Being. It is that level of cosmos that connects all, for all are within the enfolding stars. This cosmic astral plane, with its often described astral light, imprints its power by generating matrices that act upon all manifest forms, all consciousness and life. Such matrices resonate through many levels toward manifestation. For us these levels are embedded deep in our collective and individual consciousness as the realms of Stars, Sun and Planets, Moon and Earth, both physically and metaphysically.

The psychic/energetic sub-lunar realm, often incorrectly called the astral plane, enfolds planet Earth, deriving substantially (but not totally) from her Moon. It has an imprinting effect on all living creatures: it imprints them, and they mutually imprint it. Just as the Stellar forces imprint the cosmos, so do the Lunar forces imprint the sphere of Earth; think of rhythms, tides, cycles, phases, moods, sexual and breeding forces … these are but a tiny part of the forces that flow to and fro between Earth and Moon.

So this sub-lunar world, which consists of all that happens inside the sphere of influence that is shaped by the Moon orbiting around the Earth, is a miniature, a reflection or harmonic, of the astral enfoldment of the manifest universe. Furthermore, there is another minute holograph of the enfoldment within the individual human mind (this is where we return to some ideas restated by modern psychology but long known and understood by the esoteric traditions). This mirroring in miniature may be the origin of the popular misrepresentation and ignorance regarding the astral plane, and its confusion with the sub-lunar realm. It is almost certainly a mirroring of the materialistic idea of the subconscious that is found in so many books on magic and meditation today.

When we work with the Cord, we are seeking to work on the true astral plane, that realm of starry enfoldment and potentials that permeates the cosmos. This is not as abstract as it may sound, for we are already within that astral light … how could we not be?

What is the Astral Double?

Once again, we find that popular literature and fiction has taken a valid magical or spiritual concept and reduced it to confusion. Most people will tell you that an astral double is something that is built up by concentration to enable "astral travel." It is often confused with the Germanic term *doppelganger* or double-walker, which is the same as the *co-walker* of the Gaelic faery tradition. The term implies a spirit being that can mimic the human form. The *co-walker*, or *doppelganger* were never human doubles. They were faery or spirit beings who *walked with* and sometimes mimicked a human and have become confused with the idea that the human has a psychic double that can be moved around at will out of the body. None of the foregoing, either traditional folkloric or literary tale, describes the astral double, though it is easy to see how confusion arises when people simply copy such mistakes from one publication to another and never do research into definitions or origins, let alone undertake any actual practices or disciplines that bring direct experience.

Countless Astral Doubles

Anything can have an astral double ... anything at all: a nebula, a radiant sun, asteroids, a race or group being, a toaster or a crumb of toast. It is our approach to the astral doubles, our relationship and interaction with them, that enables many remarkable changes to occur. For example, what we think of in modern science as the smaller entities, such as the bacterial and microbial collectives, have substantial astral doubles en-mass. These are what we should be considering when we attempt to treat infection, rather than take a combative approach to their manifest colonies in our individual bodies. By combating them with antibiotics and other attack-orientated methods on an individual basis, we merely give the astral double means to adapt and adjust to its manifest vehicles. Or more simply, the diseases become resistant and the medications fail to work.

Some things do not have long-lasting astral doubles, many more do, and all have the potential to create or imprint doubles. Thus there are countless astral doubles: some are very short lived, others continue for millenniums, even for stellar time cycles. So let us define the astral double further and explore its nature.

Further Definition of the Astral Double

The Astral Double is a malleable imprint in the astral light in the stellar menstruum of creation. Any medieval alchemist could have told us this, or Greek philosopher, or Egyptian priestess. It took the 19th century occultists and spiritualists to distort the meaning into the neo-dogma that is so widespread today. It is a dogma that is potentially dangerous for the student, as it involves unnecessary practices to achieve ends that can be reached more easily and by safer and more beautiful and gracious methods. The reader will confirm, I am sure, most literature on so-called "astral travel" has a rather unhealthy selfish undertone whereby the traveler can gain advantage of some sort through his or her ability to "go out on the astral." This idea is really no different then spyware on a computer, and with similar degrading desires and negative end results. Alternatively it also has an ego-inflating aspect, that of the superior occultist who can fly forth and consult the astral records or overlook events at a distance. Little wonder the CIA and other intelligence services have all investigated so-called Remote Viewing. But let us discard this nonsense, and return to exploring the concept of the true astral double.

Types of Astral Double

There are many classes or types of astral double: some are small and of short duration, others are vast and enduring. At the deepest level the vast astral doubles merge with the originating archetypes of creation, and for most purposes cannot be distinguished from them in human contemplation.

It is the interaction between the large scale astral doubles and the originating archetypes of creation that gives continuity or repetition to the manifest worlds. This is a deeply significant concept for contemplation, which also has its practical applications in the sub-lunar world as we shall discover.

With our Cord work, we are concerned with something much smaller than the cosmic archetypes and their enduring astral doubles, something that is based in the same principle of imprint. We are concerned with interaction and continuity within the astral light that is the menstruum of creation.

Archetypes and Astral Doubles

Astral doubles, of any sort, can arise in more than one way. The vast doubles referred to above are those of stars or stellar groups, and are therefore of the cosmic organs of consciousness that we would probably think of, in primal human terms, as deities or perhaps in Gnostic terminology as Aeons. Remember that these are descriptive terms bound by human culture, and that none of them are perfect descriptions … *for the perfect description rests solely in contemplation of the entity that we seek to describe.* These vast doubles arise out of reflection, out of resonance, whereby the originating archetypes, that issue out of the void (Being from Non-Being), imprint the already Present astral light that radiates from earlier phases of creation. This gives a rhythmic continuity or repetition to the cosmos, though this continuity is by no means rigid and unchanging.

Archetypes or matrices of creation arise out of the Void, ceaselessly, and return to it after a cycle of manifest time/space/interaction. When they arise or are, in Qabalistic terms, Uttered, they encounter the existing astral (starry) light of previous creation, a ground or menstruum of interchangeable consciousness and energy. The same energy is described today by the abstract mathematics of quantum physics. The interaction between the archetypes and this astral menstruum generates vast imprints within the menstruum. These are cosmic astral doubles.

The same imprinting process, the same malleability of the astral light, can be used intentionally by us, in our magical arts, on our own smaller scale. How could it not be so ... are we not already within the astral light, do we not exist within the archetypes and their astral doubles?

This vast ceaseless interaction, upon a cosmic scale, is repeated right down to the microscopic levels. All life forms, all energy patterns, all consciousnesses, create an imprint in the existing astral light. This imprint tends to hold them in shape through successive manifestations or incarnations. In human life, we see this imprint in the natal chart, regardless of which tradition or method of astrology is followed. The natal chart is not so much about planetary synchronicities, as about an imprinting pattern that occurs either at conception or at birth, or, indeed, at any other given moment in the life. This imprint comes from the astral double of the solar system into the malleable field of consciousness and energy of the human, which field is, in itself, a miniature reflection of the solar system and the enfolding cosmos.

The imprint within the astral light is not, in itself, the archetype of creation that issues from the void but is a resulting impression of that archetype upon the existing astral light of creation. Eventually it can arise, so to speak, from both directions ... from the originative spirit moving Outwards towards creation, and from the manifesting consciousness moving Inwards towards the originative spirit. In either direction, it imprints the astral light or menstruum. This is one of the great "secrets" of effective magic.

IMPRINTING THE ASTRAL LIGHT

Intentional imprinting of the astral light is one of the great secrets of effective practical magic, so it is ironic, but not unexpected, that it has been trivialized in popular literature. I have no doubt that when we use the methods for establishing the Astral Double of the Cord, we are using methods that were known by the ancestral priests, priestesses, and magicians. Methods which have gradually become lost, confused, and corrupted, but which we can now reclaim for contemporary spiritual work. While I cannot offer historical proof, the widespread and enduring use of cords in spiritual and sacro-magical traditions and folkloric magic worldwide all suggest their connection to the more esoteric art that we are exploring here.

In a human life, for example, we see this astral imprint demonstrated in the natal chart, whereby a solar and planetary imprint merges with a stellar imprint at key moments, such as conception and birth. But we also see it demonstrated in the continuity of life forms in the organic world and in patterns or structures in the inorganic world.

When we enter in the metaphysical realms, the astral imprint is especially loose and malleable, as it has not yet been concretized by manifest form. Once an astral double has manifest form, it will hold together for a period of time, then as the form disintegrates, so may the astral double disintegrate through its connection to the manifest form or entity. We will return to this concept again, in the context of death and the disintegration of the body. In the astral realm however (not, please be clear, in the sub-lunar world, wherein different laws apply), the astral double can be maintained, can endure, for long periods of time, especially if this is a *conscious* action, moving in the direction away from manifesting consciousness/form towards the deeper creative realms.

All of the foregoing supports and empowers the technique that we use to maintain the astral double of the Cord. I say maintain, rather than create, because in most cases we already have the astral double of the Cord even if we are not aware of it.

CREATING AND MAINTAINING THE CORD DOUBLE

The Astral Double of your Cord is created and maintained in the Temple of Dedication, which is described and encountered in Chapter 8. We can expand this simple statement into more abstract concepts, such as it being kept at the threshold of consciousness and energy between the sub-lunar and solar and stellar worlds. The rest will come as you work with the Cord, and more insights and methods can be found in the later chapters of this book.

In Part Two, Chapter 6, on Cord Positions, we will discuss and explore some of the basic methods of holding, location, positioning and working with the Cord, that will be used in all the subsequent forms in this book. It will be of considerable help to you in your own spiritual or magical work. Before moving into Part Two, we should consider some aspects of the imagination, media use, and our ability to visualize in the context of Cord practices and our contemporary culture. Thus, Chapter 5 is essential reading before you commence your cord practices.

CHAPTER 5:
PURIFYING
THE IMAGINATION

1. The Power of the Imagination
2. Imagination and the Cord
3. Imagination and Pleasure
4. Imaginative Muscle
5. How May We Reinstate the Imagination?
6. Clarifying the Imagination
7. The Outer Disciplines and Liberations
8. The Inner Disciplines and Liberations
9. You Can't Take It With You!
10. The Secret of Powerful Visionary Work
11. In Conclusion

THE POWER OF THE IMAGINATION

If you are experienced in meditation, visualisation, and spiritual disciplines, you may feel that some of the basic information in this chapter is known to you already. It progresses from discussing some of the more obvious modern suppressions of the spiritual faculties to the more subtle, so I would encourage you to read this material thoroughly, as it contains many points that relate strongly to our Cord practices. In one sense, the contemporary magician, meditator, and spiritually aware individual should, and must, embrace the culture in which he or she lives, and a reactive rejection of it is merely weakness and lack of self knowledge. Yet we can embrace our contemporary world lightly without being enslaved, and, more significantly, with an embrace that we can disconnect and reconnect when required, according to our intention. We might express this in another way, and say that we should be very selective and use the best of modernist culture without being seduced by the worst.

This essay will also help as a reminder of the condition of the overall collective imaginative field in which we function, for this collective of imagination influences us subtly, at all times. The power of the imagination should be understood as both "internal" and "external," with loose boundaries between the two. The internal seems to be better known to us, and we think that we own it fully, though both materialist psychology and spiritual psychology caution us, in their different ways, that this is often not so, and that we must work at inner clarification . The external power of imagination that does not originate within us has two main aspects that anyone involved in spiritual disciplines must consider and explore: the first is that vast collective field of human imagining mentioned above. The second is external influence from our inner contacts, which is, or should be, at a different frequency from that of the collective. Our deeper spiritual faculties are octaves or modes of the imagination, and include deep communication, initiation of subtle changes, and perception of metaphysical reality through the mediation of our inner contacts. If the imagination is clouded, this second "external" interaction cannot reach us or function adequately.

IMAGINATION AND THE CORD

The sacro-magical Cord is empowered at many levels by our imagination. Not the imagination as fantasy, but as our creative spiritual faculty, as a working tool that we may use in a focussed and disciplined manner.

This concept is, in itself, difficult for modern people, as the imagination is typically seen as a source of relaxation, entertainment, and fantasy, which indeed it can be, quite appropriately at certain times and in certain circumstances. Often it is employed solely for such purposes and for nothing more; with the high visual content and powerful audio of entertainment media, the imagination is loaded, so to speak, with manipulated external images and associated sounds, and seldom has the opportunity to generate clear and fresh images for itself. Furthermore, media images tend to supplant and eventually destroy an older stratum of mythic images handed down from our ancestral collectives of consciousness. In most contemporary people, these ancestral levels are either deeply buried, supplanted, or absent. They can be recovered in conscious meditation and attunement, and many contemporary practices in the current spiritual/magical revival pay attention to such recovery. In the folkloric traditions of many ethnic cultures, this ancestral level is still active and potent, of course, and has never been lost or forgotten.

Imagination and Pleasure

If we limit the imagination to playing in the vast pleasure house of modern media, or to compulsive fantasies, then we use it only for its most trivial functions of self-gratification and entertainment, and we risk losing one of our most powerful magical tools, and the atrophy one of our most far reaching spiritual faculties. The imagination, when it is given solely to fantasy can lead us into artificial worlds, artificial and delusory lives and we can harm both ourselves and others thereby. This phenomenon seems very prevalent today through the internet, where individuals can indulge in creating fantasy identities and lives in communication with one another. At one level this is merely pathetic, but as it strengthens through habit it becomes compulsive and dangerous in both the outer and inner worlds.

Imaginative Muscle

The imagination, in our sub-lunar world, is somewhat like a muscle which must be used and nourished to be strong. It has to be exercised in a healthy and balanced way, and appropriately nourished with spiritual input. The inverse of this healthy nourishment is widespread, of course, for just as we can build unnatural musculature through programs using equipment and steroids, so can we build an unnatural imagination through the use of media equipment, of drugs, of vicious entertainment, compulsive fantasy, sexually addictive habits, and pornography.

It is the vitalising of the imaginative muscle, in the sub-lunar world, that gives us the necessary strength for the clarification and special use of the imagination that we can develop in the Over and Under Worlds. Therefore much of what is discussed here deals with the cleansing, nourishment and development of the imaginative muscle that we use to move ourselves into the greater spiritual imagination. Further clarification and transformation of the imagination, at the deeper levels, is achieved through spiritual disciplines, such as meditation, visualisation, ritual, and through the Cord forms offered in our other chapters.

How May We Reinstate the Imagination?

It may seem like a hopeless task to reinstate the spiritual imagination in a culture that perpetually degrades it through media and commercial manipulation. Yet, with a few small changes, and some steady discipline, we can free up from the subtle, and not so subtle, chains and addictions that are so continuously laid upon us. Addictions which, it must be said, we willingly accept, allow, and even encourage in ourselves and in one another. Understanding our ongoing acceptance of imaginative degradation is a hard task, for many things that are regarded as normal and even harmless in modern culture can be damaging to our spiritual faculties and inner integrity. Many people who practise meditative traditions within magical arts, spiritual disciplines, paganism and witchcraft are still shocked by, for example, the suggestion that they should not watch television.

On the positive side of the scales is the essential understanding that the imagination changes and develops exponentially when we clarify it. To degrade the imagination takes steady repeated steps, which, nowadays, begins even in childhood with television and computer gaming. To nourish and clarify the imagination, we find that continued steady effort makes huge changes rapidly, after an initially difficult readjustment phase. The readjustment phase can be likened to a fast and an internal cleanse, which needs commitment and resolution to succeed. But after this fast comes wholesome nourishment, and then we see surprisingly powerful results (providing we do not poison our imagination again).

This is so because when we clarify the imagination it returns to its natural state, which is far more vibrant and alive than the degraded imagery and entertainment level within which it is so often imprisoned. Our imagination can return home, and the Cord work greatly assists with this return.

CLARIFYING THE IMAGINATION

If we read some of the classic sources of spiritual teaching from earlier centuries, we find that clarifying the imagination was dependent upon inner observation. This is well known in traditions such as mystical Christianity, Buddhism, Islam, Judaism, and so forth. Today we have a huge additional task, welded heavily onto that of inner observation. Indeed, we cannot pursue clear inner observation until we have completely detached our consciousness from this welded weight, which accumulates subtly and inexorably from external media stimulus. Such stimulus comes from computers, television, film, radio, and (to a lesser extent) newspapers and magazines.

Here are some basic ground rules for clarifying the imagination, especially with regard to spiritual awareness and the Cord. You may already be following some of these rules, of course, while others may be new to you. Even you are already practising some or all of the simple disciplines listed here, you may find some new ideas or insights, especially from the perspective of your Cord work.

The Outer Disciplines and Liberations

1. Television: *Do not watch television!* Do not have television on "in the background," and never (never) go to sleep with television on, never watch it from bed in the bedroom ... do not have a television set or media player in the bedroom. For media entertainment select good films, go out to a theatre, or watch them on video or DVD, but otherwise keep the TV off. Ideally get rid of it, watch your films on that essential tool of modern life, your computer ... we will return to the computer shortly. *Do not watch television!*

If you are serious about your spiritual/magical work, television is your enemy. This may sound dramatic ... most people have several televisions at home ... so what? In our context of the imagination, television is a pollutant. It presents images externally, which become imprinted, often through repetition. What we put into the imagination shapes that which comes out. At this stage in the exploration we are not talking about *content*, but only about flashing images, strongly reinforced by sounds and music. We will discuss content shortly.

Once the imagination becomes accustomed to receiving input from television, there is an addictive pattern. People feel lonely, isolated, and cut off without television. The next stage is the "always on" stage, when the television is left on for "background" or "company" or "just in case there is anything I want to watch." The individual has lost the ability to choose, to switch off the machine. As parents know, teenagers become obsessed with television, computer games, and the internet. But this addiction is found in millions of adults also, including many who meditate and are involved in spiritual practices.

Do not have television on "in the background," and never (never) go to sleep with the television on, or even with it (off) in the bedroom.

As much as half of our life is spent in sleep: many important things happen while we sleep, and spiritual transformation and regeneration occurs during this time, just as much as in waking meditations, visions, or ceremony. Indeed, many of the things we do, as spiritual disciplines, are furthered in our sleep when we pass out through the sub-lunar realm in dreams, to reach into the solar realm momentarily before making the return passage to the outer world of nature and human everyday life.

If television is watched shortly before sleeping, the flashing images replay and condition what occurs in sleep. If you go to sleep with the television on low, as many people do, it will continue to influence you during your sleep … you will absorb the images, the content, and the frequencies. You cannot make a choice … you are asleep. Some people cannot sleep without it on low … they are addicted. If you have a television in the house, consider throwing it out. But no matter what you do with it, never have one in the bedroom.

Television content: There are three aspects of content that are deleterious to the imagination. (1) Actual subject matter, as discussed above. Be selective on your subject matter, and be active. Television is a passive receptive medium; we sit and watch, receive, absorb, become loaded with, and eventually highly influenced by, the content. (2) The wide range of content offered is, in itself, destructive to the imagination and spiritual faculties. With many channels to choose from, the television and cable addict becomes a channel surfer … he or she shrinks into a short attention span, and flips across myriad content moment by moment. (3) Television as an organ of propaganda and commercial manipulation. Be choosy, and opt not to accept, but to research (you cannot do active research on a subject on television, you have to take it or leave it). *For media enter-tainment, select good films, go out to a theatre, or watch them on video or DVD, but otherwise keep the TV off.*

2. Entertainment: Be very choosey. Do not watch anything vicious or sexually unhealthy, either in film or on the Internet. Understand that the images that you feed into your imagination will change your consciousness. If you feed degraded or unhealthy images and fantasies into your imagination, you will become unhealthy mentally, emotionally, and physically. Every organ in the body responds to the condition of the imagination, so you must be very cautious about what you feed into it and store in it. This is not to be "puritanical" but only to be clear, balanced, and healthy.

3. Drugs and alcohol. No recreational drugs. Alcohol in moderation or not at all. No smoking (anything). The only exception would be sacred tobacco if that is your true cultural tradition and if you have a deep affinity with, and understanding of, its sacredness.

4. Reading: do not read trivial magazines and popular newspapers. Do not read books that deliberately exploit and promote violence or unhealthy sexual images, or degraded images of monsters, vampires, perversion, torture, and so forth.

5. Online: this is the biggest medium and organ of communication and everyone is using it. The Internet, the Web. It can be of immense value in finding quality news (no need for that television newscaster yapping constantly, invading your house with his or her obtrusive presence!). The internet is useful for finding information, for research, for purchasing, and for many other things. But it has a dark unhealthy side, the world of fantasy, lies, violence and pornography. Be very selective with your content.

There is an addictive aspect to just being on line, even for the most simple uses such as email. If you find that you spend a long time on line, set yourself a timetable and keep to it strictly. Ideally a reducing timetable, whereby you cut down your time online progressively over a few weeks. There is no need to cut it out altogether, unless you are truly ready to do so, and are able to live and work without it. As mentioned above, we can, and should, embrace modern culture lightly, without being ensnared and enslaved by it.

All of the five points above are both personal disciplines and cultural disciplines that are essentially for healthy living today. It is not possible to have clear inner observation and a healthy imagination until those five steps have been implemented, upheld, and rigorously maintained. There can be no going backward on these five, if you wish to progress and transform your spiritual life.

THE INNER DISCIPLINES AND LIBERATIONS

6. Fantasies in human interaction: this is a more subtle aspect of the imagination, for you have to observe your fantasies as they arise. This is done when you are *not* involved in media entertainment, but in human interaction. What do you imagine about the people around you ... how much of your interaction is based upon imagination? The answer is, almost all of it. Observe your reactions and interactions with others, and look for the imaginative fantastical elements. Would you bring them out into the open and speak them aloud or act upon them? This is probably the key test for how your imagination works, and how healthy it is.

Once again, this is not about being "superior" or purist in a religious dogmatic sense; it is merely about discovering how you use your imagination. This observation of the imagination, and clarification according to what is discovered, should be an essential aspect of your human relationships, with loved ones, family, associates, and so forth. It is especially enlightening when we choose to explore it in relationships, intimacy, and love. Sometimes the delusion of love is preferred to the presence of love, and our contemporary media, especially the internet, and email, tends to reinforce and enable such delusions. The creation of an "alternative" personality and acting a fantasy life through it was, until recently, considered an indicator of imbalance or potential dysfunction, yet the internet and email have made such fragmentation and dysfunction into daily practice for millions.

The dictum of the Mysteries has always been "Human, know yourself." The dictum of online communication is "never reveal who you are, even to yourself."

7. Solitary daydreams, reveries, and fantasies: Another essential element is to observe your daydreams and fantasies that arise when you are alone. If you have practiced meditation, you will know that an endless torrent of thoughts, speculations, daydreams, fantasies and spontaneous images can, and does, flow freely. Part of basic meditative disciplines is not to fight this torrent, but to observe and acknowledge it, then be still. The patterns come, they go, but you are still.

The seven disciplines, five external and two internal, interact continuously with one another. If you can achieve the first five, then you will find the two inner disciplines possible. If you fail in just one of the first five, you will never be able to follow the internal disciplines that clarify the imagination.

We might conclude this short exploration by considering this thought: when you practice the disciplines listed above, you are claiming back that which is rightfully yours ... you sacred imagination, your clarity, your integrity, your ability to love and communicate as your true self, free of influences, delusions, manipulations, propaganda, and compulsions. Why would we not wish to do this? What trivial cyber-zone could possibly imprison us when we choose to claim ourselves, know ourselves, be ourselves?

You Can't Take It With You!

Here we should remind ourselves again that the computer is an electrically powered tool. While there is much shrill praise for its supposedly analogous "consciousness," you cannot take it into the realms of consciousness and spirit. Nor can the Internet become a realm of living consciousness, as has been suggested repeatedly. Consciousness continues after death, but a computer has no functional ability after the plug is pulled. You cannot take your laptop,

PDA, or cell-phone into the spiritual worlds: they are inert machines dependant upon electricity. We should also remember that the best a computer can do is find and organise data rapidly, and all other presentations such as graphics, sound, interactive appearances, derive from this data organisation ... this is not consciousness, it is merely functional sorting.

While you cannot take calculating machines into the spiritual realms, you can and do take your own living consciousness. Therefore the freer we become of any tool that inhibits awareness and makes us dependent upon it to function in our outer life, the more conscious we will be in meditation, after death and at rebirth. Our Cord practices reduce all aids and tools down to one simple cord ... and then to the astral imprint of that cord: Freedom.

Having focussed on negative aspects of imaginative power in our contemporary culture, let us move on to a positive method that greatly enhances our visionary work, both with the Cord forms, and with all spiritual visualisation, regardless of content or tradition. If you use the method described next as the basis or foundation method for all the Cord forms in this book, you will receive many benefits and insights.

THE SECRET OF POWERFUL VISIONARY WORK

Always build the vision *before* you. Do not conceive it as something inside your skull, only a fantasy, limited to your own inner imaginings.

Build a picture of your chosen vision, subject and/or scenario in front of you ... approximately at arms length. In some instances build the vision behind or around the sacred candle flame, or on or beyond a wall. Such is the core of a "secret" technique that will make your visionary work powerful, and which will continue to develop and grow within you.

In other words, it is projected outwards, rather than being limited to something inside your head. This inside-the-head notion is extremely limiting and enervating. If you regard your sacro-magical visions in this way you are succumbing to a materialist interpretation of magic and imagination ... it is all in the mind; it has no reality. But if you see, sense, and feel the visionary scenario before you, separate from your body, it becomes intense and alive. Furthermore, other beings can share in this, ranging from fellow humans, faery allies, angels, transhuman mentors, and many more. It becomes a group structure.

Using this hallowed method might also help to dispose of the classic modernist question "Is it all in my own mind?" No, it is not, for you work with the visionary scenario before you, rather than inside the skull and brain.

It might be argued that this method fosters illusion, but you need only think of television or computer entertainment, wherein the content is driven and manipulated externally to discover where illusion proliferates. With *empowered vision*, we work with a property or metaphysical law, to shape the spiritual energies. This type of active, projected, vision is similar to moulding clay. Indeed, the ground, or substance that we mould by such methods is the ground of the sub-lunar realm, that realm between Moon and Earth that holds the precursors of form as form develops out of consciousness (see Chapters 4 and 9 for further discussion of the sub-lunar realm).

This way of working is a specialised form, yet it is firmly based on the every day manner in which we hold the so-called "real" world together. This "real" world is a combination of many perceptions of the ground of being, manifesting in a multitude of shared modes and presentations. It is a consensual world. Yet is also many shared worlds and many different worlds intersecting with another. We know, for example, that the world perceived by an ant is different from the world perceived by a human, yet both are in a third, shared, world. No doubt they are in many other worlds also, according to how the ant, the human, and the worlds, conceive of one another. This property of being where the ground or field can be selectively perceived is employed intentionally in magic.

We find it extensively in the temple art of the ancient world, and in the imagery of icons and temple art of contemporary traditional cultures. While monotheists fear that the images or idols will become false objects of worship, the esotericist understands that they act as gateways for spiritual consciousness and presence. This is achieved by externalising the individual awareness, so that he or she interacts with the sacred image that is presented in artistic form. When a group does this, or when it has been done repeatedly for years, often times centuries, the interaction can be extremely powerful. Some images of deities are attuned strongly to the power of that deity and are by no means symbols or clues for meditation or prayer or worship. They are transtemporal and interdimensional gateways for the power of the deity depicted.

In our cord work, we do not use statues or pictures extensively, though there is no prohibition on using them. Be aware, however, that if you use cultural images, or religious images, in iconic form, that they will bring with them the power and burden of that god, goddess, religion, or culture. As a rule, in cord work, we do not work with cultural or historical deities and concretized images, for that reason. We seek, instead, the spiritual powers behind and beyond those cultural or historical images, and encounter them directly, through the mediating qualities of our cords.

When you use this method of envisioning the subject before you (rather than in your skull), there is always a threshold that is crossed when the imagery changes from being a construct to a metaphysical experience. When you cross that threshold, it becomes real and takes on a vitality and substance that cannot be denied or explained away by psychological reductionism. I have seen many people cross this threshold in group work, and, interestingly, it can be the sceptic or open-minded materialist who crosses it more easily than the believer. Believers often carry a huge amount of dogma and baggage from New Age or neo-pagan modern practices. Sometime this baggage contains useful tools, but it can also obscure our vision and weigh us down. This is why, of course, we all experience moments when we discover that we have outgrown the magical or spiritual practices of one phase of our lives, and are ready to move on. We have shed some baggage at this point, and though it was useful for the early stages of the journey, it can be disposed of, recycled, and let go.

In Conclusion

Chapter 5 is the pivotal chapter in this book. It marks the transition from exposition and metaphysical exploration, to our practical Cord Forms. By this stage the reader should be ready for practical work with his or her cord. If you are concerned regarding some of the prohibitions suggested in this Chapter and find that they may apply to you, have a media fast before you start work with the Cord Forms. Take 10 days with no television, and allow yourself to go online only every second or third day for one hour only. If your job involves online work, as many do, cut out time online at home completely during your media fast.

After your media fast, work out your own program for reduction of online time, and throw out your TV. If your television is used only for watching films through DVD or video, cancel your cable or satellite subscription and take down your aerial. You will be amazed at the time and money that you save.

Part Two

Introduction to Part Two

From this stage on our intense practical work begins. You will be working with both the text and the CD towards the empowerment of your Cord. In Chapter 6 we describe the basic cord positions that may be used in practical work.

The empowerment of the cord goes through three initiatory stages, which are triggered by the three forms in the following chapters: 7 The Crossroads / 8 The Temple of Dedication / 9 The Lunar Realm. In Chapter 10, we explore further Cord Forms, while in Chapter 11 we consider the Cord of Death.

What does "empowerment" mean in the context of the Cord? It is not empowerment in a personal, political, or egocentric sense. It is the weaving of certain spiritual powers into the physical cord. It is the Cord that is empowered, not the personality. Such powers may be both *energies* and *entities*. Indeed, in some cases the energy is delivered to the Cord by entities, such as the faery allies at the Crossroads, the mentoring spirits in the Temple of Dedication, or the angelic beings in the Lunar Realm. In other cases, it is the subtle energies in the Cord that enable us to open and maintain inner contacts and work with spiritual entities. Eventually you will find that energies and entities are interchangeable but do not fall into an intellectual trap of comparisons. Experience and participation is all. Mental comparisons (is it an entity or is it an energy?) are of little value.

The three stages that follow begin in the UnderWorld and Faery Realm, at the Crossroads. Then continue at the threshold between the world of nature (our outer world, but including the UnderWorld and Faery Realm) and the OverWorld of Moon, Sun and Stars. This Threshold is the Temple of Dedication, where Above and Below meet, at the summit of the sacred mountain. The third stage is that of the Gold and Silver Stairs, which carries us, with our Cords, into the Lunar Realm and ultimately into the Solar Realm.

At each stage, something is woven into the Cord. This "something" connects our physical cord to the metaphysical energies and entities, the places and people of the spiritual dimensions. And eventually it nourishes our astral cord ... the double that we rediscover and claim in the Temple of Dedication.

After the three initiatory forms have been undertaken in order (working the threefold cycle at least three times!) we progress to other Cord forms in Chapter 10, such as Distance Contact, Moon Sun and Stars Communion, Fishing in the Well of Light and, in Chapter 11, the Cord of Death.

On then, to the Crossroads!

Chapter 6:
CORD POSITIONS

1. Cord Positions
2. Cord Positions in Three Modes
3. Positions in Still Meditation
4. Positions Within Visualization
5. Positions in Ritual
6. Positions at Rest

CORD POSITIONS

The following is a basic list of cord positions and some of the uses that they have. You will find others as you work with your cord. The cord itself will teach you, as will many of the inner contacts that you will make in meditation and vision, especially in the defined Inner Temples and at the Crossroads. Become familiar with these basic cord positions; practice them frequently individually, even if the practice is brief. You will also find them within the longer *forms* in the other chapters, and you will be able to use them to create your own *forms*.

CORD POSITIONS IN THREE MODES

1. Positions in still *meditation*: these are usually seated, but may also be standing. Our customary idea of meditation is that of a seated

practice with eyes closed. However, standing meditations or meditations with eyes open are equally effective, and in some contexts more powerful. Walking meditations with eyes open are included in mode 3.

2. Positions within *visualization*: in this method, the physical positions are employed while you are "inside" a vision. They are not imagined, but are carried out in the outer world physically with your cord and body. They can also be carried out using the cord together with other objects (such as an altar, a stone, a tree, and so forth).

3. Positions within *ritual*. This is similar in physical practice to mode 2, but the cord is used as a ritual tool within the overall pattern of the ritual or ceremony. We can include in this third set the practice of *walking meditation*, as this is also a ritual.

We can add a fourth mode, which is when the cord is "at rest." This can be as simple as keeping the cord in small bag when you are traveling, or placing it upon the meditation altar at home when you are engaged in the activities of daily life.

ESSENTIAL NOTE: *the cord should stay with you or on your altar at all times*. When you are traveling, keep it in a small soft bag in your pocket or personal purse or bag. Never check it into baggage handling or storage. If you are at work, keep it close by in your pocket or purse.

If you are at home, keep it on a meditation altar using one of the key positions or patterns described here (such as around a central candle stone or bowl). You can also lay it out in a pattern you find in meditation, drawn with the twists or curves of the cord. If you are going out briefly, you can leave it on the altar if you wish ... there is no need to be obsessive about keeping it on your body.

SLEEP: as mentioned elsewhere, *sleep with your cord*. Do not neglect this practice, for much comes from it.

a. At the least, sleep with it under your pillow, either in a soft bag or without a bag.

b. You can opt to sleep with it in your hand, coiled around or simply bundled.
c. Sleeping with the cord across your lower body/navel is very effective. You can hold the right and left ends or leave it loose.
d. Coiled around one or both arms. However, this tends to be disruptive of sleep due to the energetic boost that it gives.
e. Around the back of the neck, ends over the front of your body. Only do this for very deep work.

POSITIONS IN STILL MEDITATION

These are some of the typical positions for the cord, in either seated or standing meditation. You will discover others for yourself. The positions and general use are summarized here, and you will find examples in our various longer *cord forms* and other workings throughout the book.

1. The center point of your cord is at and around the back of your neck, with the cord passing over your shoulders to the front of your body. The ends may fall loose or be held in each hand (Figure 1). Use this position when you are working with powerful known or unknown spiritual forces, or when you wish to be connected to the "off-planet" spiritual streams. This position is greatly enhanced by practicing the form of *Moon, Sun and Stars* found in Chapter 9.
Use this cord position thoughtfully and sparingly, and be sure to use the other cord positions for their appropriate tasks. There is a tendency for people to insist on using the "most powerful" whenever possible. This is a serious error, similar to running your toaster with a furnace or fitting your bicycle with a high powered racing car engine. The secret of all magic is *appropriate power in balance,* not maximum power in and of itself. This same law of balance and proportion is found in all the physical skills, which is why the old traditions required that the magician or mystic also work with his or her hands in a craft. Misplaced power is a source of weakness and imbalance in all things. Therefore, the magician or mystic learns skills such as metal work, gardening, weaving and

wood carving. Such crafts teach us the appropriate use and relevant level of power in action: too little and you cannot create what you intend, too much and you destroy it.

2. The center point of the cord is behind and around you on the lower spine, with most of the cord around the waist. The cord should be tied with a loose knot and let the ends simply fall. Alternatively your hands can hold each end or hold both ends together in one hand (Figure 2, 2a). Use this position when you are in ritual, vision or meditation where you need balance and support. This is the classic cord position known in many versions worldwide using cords, prayer beads, sacred strings, wraps or shawls, whereby you wear the cord invisibly under clothing or visibly around a ritual robe or in a ceremony. This is also practical for a walking meditation where the cord is not seen by others.

3. The center point of the cord is across and in the center of your lap while seated. The ends may fall loose or may be held (Figure 3). Use this position for seated meditation and visionary work. This could be described as a semi-open position, as your cord has some protecting and containing qualities. This position is especially useful when exploring new inner contacts at a simple and moderate level of working.

4. The cord is upheld before you in both hands with arms somewhat apart (Figure 4). Use this when offering up the cord to spiritual contacts and energies in readiness for it to be empowered or charged. This might be regarded as a *passive* or receptive form, or an *offering* form, or as a form showing willingness to *exchange*.

5. The cord is partly coiled around both arms with ends in your hands and the centre of the cord hanging in front of your body. You should have free arm movement vertically up or down but limited movement horizontally, as the cord will pull tight (Figure 5). This is a more powerful form of (4) but is always used as an *active* cord position. This form may be used for invocation or evocation and for lending strength to sacro-magical actions involving the hands and arms.

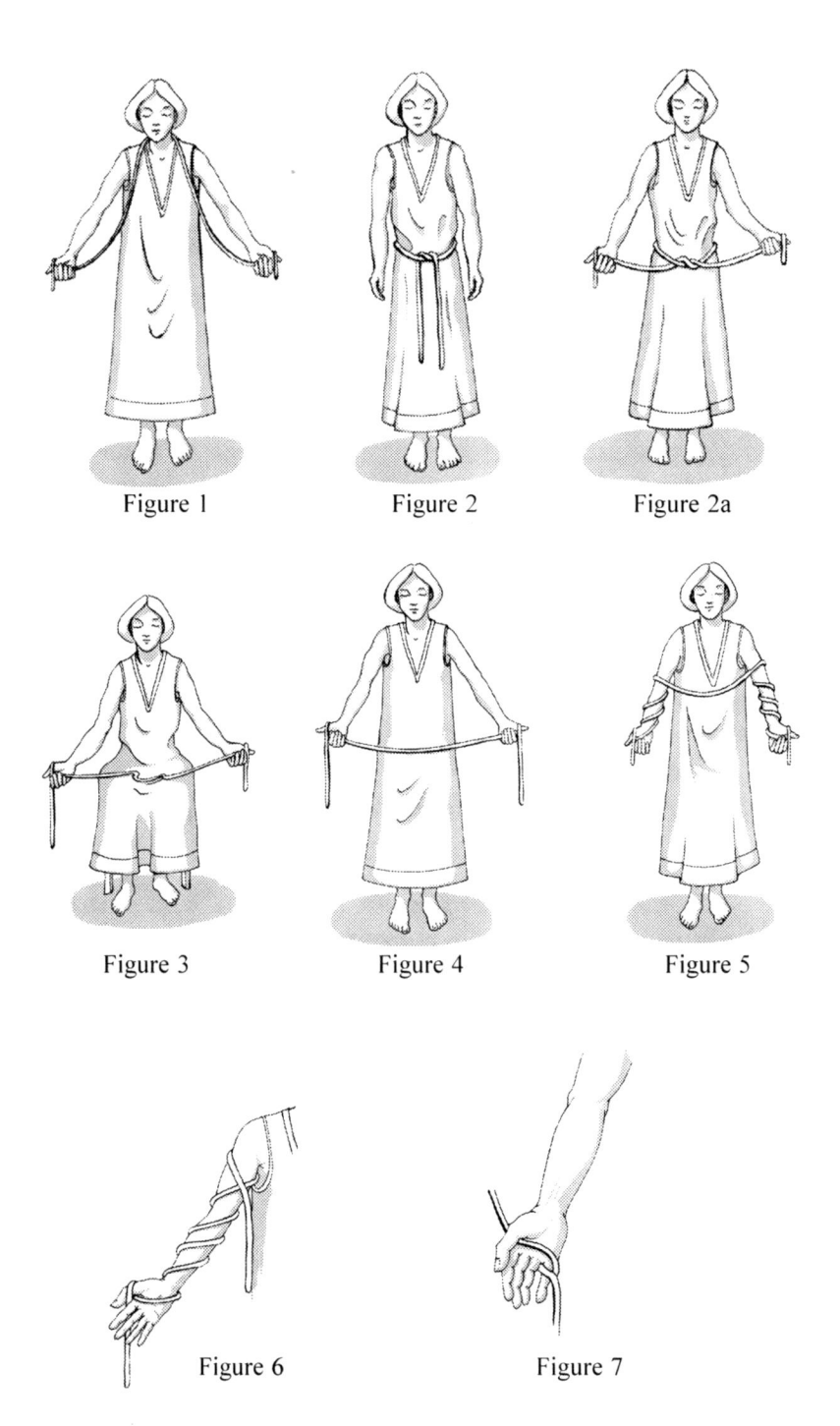

CORD POSITIONS 77

Figure 1

Figure 2

Figure 2a

Figure 3

Figure 4

Figure 5

Figure 6

Figure 7

6. The cord is coiled around one arm, upper end on the upper arm with the lower end in your hand (Figure 6). This is the *serpent* form and is used for protection of others, for purity of energy in a ritual, for giving forth power to others and/or in a ritual context. It may also be used for specific blessings which flow from the hand and may be coiled on either the right of left hand. You will discover which is best for you in general practice.

7. The ends of cord may also be coiled once around little fingers, or around the thumbs. (Figure 7). You can use this in all general use and in positions that allow for it. This gives a boost to your subtle forces when you are doing any spiritual, magical or inner work. Like all energetic boosts, be they plant induced or metaphysically communed, use it sparingly and try to work without it whenever you can. Otherwise its special effect becomes dissipated.

8. With your cord around neck or waist, the ends are placed upon an altar or other special locus. This is often used in a ritual context whereby the cord reaches into a specific source of spiritual power or a specific location such as an Inner Temple. In this form, the center of the cord upholds you through your body while the ends connect to the metaphysical dimensions bringing the power through into your body.

9. Holding the ends in your right and left hands, the middle of the cord is placed on an altar or passed around a stone, a tree or a ritual object for meditation. In this form, the center of the cord connects you to another locus, power or contact while you hold the ends. Note that 8 and 9 are *polarized variations* of one another. You should work with both but, as a learning process, use the same object, contact or metaphysical connection. Try it with each position in turn. Discover how they work differently for you and within you.

10. Holding one end of your cord, the other end extends along the ground. This line of connection can touch an object or it can lead like a life-line or conduit into another realm of being. An example is our *Well of Light* working (Chapter 10).

POSITIONS WITHIN VISUALIZATIONS

This method is extremely useful. While in a visionary form (i.e. visualizing an Inner Temple or at the Crossroads), physical cord positions and movements are undertaken. The outer cord is used in the inner dimension and the outer simultaneously.

The typical positions 1-10 listed above are used while inside a visionary working or visualization. The content and inner contacts of the place, temple or location work with you and your cord. A typical example is the "offering up" or "making visible" of your Great Cord at the Crossroads, which is described in Chapter 6.

POSITIONS IN RITUAL

In ritual work, pattern-making is paramount. Powerful rituals are sparse with words but rich in magical pattern making and communion with spiritual beings through the patterns. In ritual, the cord may be used in the following ways:

1. As an overall empowering cord located around the neck or the waist. In this mode, occasional use is made of the ends of the cord, tying, looping, placing, linking and so forth.

2. As a ritual implement that is not worn. In highly attuned ritual forms, the cord can be used off the body for pattern making on an altar, for defined power-shapes on the ground and to create thresholds, linkages and (as in traditional folkloric magic) for shaping a circle. In this context (10) listed above is useful as the cord connects the outer world of the ritual to the inner world along its length. The ritualist may hold one end and spirit contacts hold the other.

POSITIONS AT REST

Remember that you can and should rest. When you are relaxed and doing something mundane, leave the cord in its bag or on the altar. You do not need it to watch a film or to go out for dinner with a friend. Loosing is as powerful as Binding.

Now that you have read through and rehearsed the basic Cord Positions, you are ready to move on to the main practices and forms. This will begin the cycle of empowerment and initiation that begins at the Crossroads, expands in the Temple of Dedication, and climbs the Gold and Silver Stairs.

Chapter 7:
THE CROSSROADS

1. The First Weaving into the Cord
2. Aims of the Crossroad Form
3. Cords Great and Small
4. Small Cords in Tradition
5. Great Cords in Tradition
6. Making the Cord Visible or Invisible
7. The Crossroads Form

The First Weaving into the Cord

All magic, all spirit, all life and death, begins and ends at the Crossroads. The center of the Crossroads is where the Directions come together and from whence they emanate. It is where all transformations arise, where all journeys commence, and where we pause awhile before taking new directions. A Crossroads can be in any physical location and it can, as we all know, manifest forcefully in our outer lives when decisions must be made. We are often most aware when life decisions are forced upon us by circumstances. A major aspect of magic is to learn how to participate consciously in changes long before they manifest themselves in the outer life as a crisis at the Crossroads. For that alone working with a Cord of connection at the Crossroads is invaluable to us, providing we truly wish to participate that connection rather than passively escape into the oblivion of drugs, media, and entertainment that substitutes for life in modernist culture.

In folkloric magic the crossroads played, and still play, a major role either as a physical crossroads where trails meet or as a confluence of streams or rivers. In ancestral magic people worked at powerful locations which are marked in many lands by single standing stones. In Britain and Europe such stones, often dating from the time of the ancestral megalithic culture, eventually became milestones or crosses.

Before we explore the first weaving of the Crossroads Form, let us examine the inner, or metaphysical, nature of our task.

Aims of the Crossroad Form

In this first weaving, our aim is to establish communion with the faery realm and with the spiritual creatures of the many orders of life on our planet. Traditionally, humans and others meet at the Crossroads. In this instance, we are intentionally working with our Cords – taking them to the Crossroads. It is the use of the physical cord that defines the type of spiritual magic that is opened out. This physical cord must not be omitted or bypassed for without it the spiritual forces will not come fully through into the outer world.

Cords Great and Small

Typically you will work with two kinds of cord: great and small. Great Cords are your own height, made of a strong but supple woven material. Ideally this should be organic rather than synthetic, but this is not a firm rule. The material used usually does not affect the spiritual forces, though we should have many ethical reasons why we would prefer organic cord. The type of fine woven cord that you find in an upholstery or craft store is often used, if you buy your cord. Many people buy strands and weave the Cord themselves by plaiting the strands. Traditional colors for the Cord are Red, White, and Black. You can use a single color, or weave all three. You can likewise use whatever color appeals to you or inspires you. The Cord should neither be too thick, nor as thin as a single string.

The Great Cord should be simple: tie off or bind each end in plain and workmanlike manner, and avoid complex knots or decorations. Why? Because spiritual forces are woven into the cord, so additions, if any, may come later as a result of those forces. From a practical perspective, the cord should be easy to coil up and put away, into a small carrying pouch. If it is festooned with amulets, crystals, bones, beads, feathers and hubcaps, this may be difficult. Remember, the Cord is supposed to be anonymous and invisible.

SMALL CORDS IN TRADITION

In faery tradition, working with the Cord and cords is well known. Ancestral magic used small cords in many ways: they were sometimes tied around a wrist or ankle, as temporary cords for special purposes. Such temporary cords were also tied to trees, usually for supplication, or to door handles, or posts and timbers at a threshold, or inside a house. In folkloric magic, you may make many small cords for short term purposes, but you will most likely only make one Great Cord. Note: use caution when tying cords to trees; be sure that the cord will rapidly biodegrade. Synthetics or tough cords will constrict and damage the tree as it grows. The idea is, always, that the small cord has a limited life, and after it has served its purpose, is taken down. In practice, a small cord will often break or fall off its location once its work is done but you should also be responsible in the choice of material and the tying.

GREAT CORDS IN TRADITION

The Great Cord (this is not a term found in tradition but is helpful to us in contemporary work), was a length of cord that was used for all forms of magic and was kept hidden. It is sometimes difficult for modern readers to grasp how utterly subjugated our ancestors were in their sharply divided culture of masters and servants or slaves. By this I do not mean the African slaves, whose story is well known, but the white slaves in Europe, and in America where Irish or Scottish slaves were used in the thousands to establish the Colonies.

It is known that in Britain and Europe, the peasants' houses were subject to search at any time and many items were forbidden on pain of serious punishment. And this is apart from the deportation and slavery issues. Confiscations, either according to the rules of the time, or according to whim of the searchers, were frequent. British and European peasants were not allowed to keep or use refined weapons of any sort, as these were the sole property of the ruling classes. This simple historical fact calls into question the origin of the popular modern idea of the *athamé* in witchcraft, though this does not, of course, question its validity or efficacy in magical ritual. Any dedicated ritual knife would be subject to confiscation, and very difficult to hide in a peasant village situation. It seems more likely that a very plain dull kitchen knife might have been used, rather than a decorated dagger.

At various times in British and European history, there were serious penalties for having, holding or hiding, a weapon. Of course there were! The ruling classes enforced their rule at the point of the sword. So the sword was not a ritual implement for the majority, only for the upper classes.

But a cord ... a piece of rope or twine, had no value. Little wonder, then, that the primal faery tradition used cords so widely. The cord was, in effect, invisible to the dominant ruling class and to their enforcers. It could be in full view tied around a sack and attract no attention.

Making the Cord Invisible or Visible

Our aim is to go to the Crossroads with our Great Cord, and to make it apparent, visible, tangible and present to the faery allies and spiritual creatures. In general practice the Cord should be invisible in the outer world but highly visible in the inner worlds. When we do this, we are participating in a form of magic that has been known and practiced for many centuries. The spirit beings know and recognize our intentions when we do this.

There are several levels of work with the Cord and, though you may do any or all of them, in practice the power of the Cord builds strongly if an "organic" sequence is used. That is our aim in this practical manual, to build the spiritual forces of the Cord from their Foundation in the faery realm at the Crossroads to their Crown of spiritual illumination in the starry cosmos.

This sequence begins with the faery realm and spiritual creatures, the closest spiritual world to our outer world of Nature. In this way a foundation for the power of the Cord is established aiding us in our reach into other spiritual dimensions. In the later stages of weaving power into the Cord, we will work with the angelic and archangelic realms and with the Inner Temples. But it all rests upon the foundation of faery magic which integrates the spiritual forces through into the natural world. We will explore this process in several ways throughout the following chapters, as it is essential to our task.

Let us proceed now to the Crossroads:

THE CROSSROADS FORM

An earlier version of this form is also found in *The Well of Light*, in the context of faery healing, but without the Cord practices. As with all sacro-magical forms, the basic pattern of the Crossroads remains constant but what happens there changes according to our intention and our allotted tasks.

This is the pattern of the Crossroads that forms and empowers your Great Cord: in practice it will often change according to your location. The Crossroads can be on the plains, in the mountains, by the seashore, in the desert and/or in the middle of the big city. They can be anywhere where the Seven Directions and the Four Hidden Ways come together.

Coming into the Directions

Begin by being still. Still your sense of Time and Space, and cease all Movement but for Breath, in and out.

Be aware first and last of the Sky Above, and the Land Below; and of the Directions of the Land, which are East, South, North, and West. So you have a Direction behind you, and a Direction before you, and to your Right and to your Left. The Direction behind you flows through you and moves you forward. The Direction Before you flows to you and creates according to your movement. Those on your Right and Left strengthen and uphold you.

Now you have a sense of Place, of the Center of your true home which is neither Here nor There, but at the Heart of the Four Directions.

The Crossroads

Find yourself at the Crossroads, where the Four Hidden Ways come together. The Four Hidden Ways of the World that make long journeys short and short ways heavy with unimagined time. The Hidden Ways that pass through all places, all times, all events, secret and concealed, yet open and visible to all who have eyes to see and hearts to feel.

The Crossroads is an open place with four plain simple tracks or ways meeting in the Center. They come, all four, to the central stone which is a small upright stone carved with spiral patterns.

The Hidden Way of the East leads to the endless grassy plains rippling in the Wind. The Hidden Way of the South leads to the White Hill crowned with radiant trees in the place of Light. The Hidden Way of the North leads to the dark ancient forests and the Sacred Mountain. The Hidden Way of the West leads to the murmuring realm of the ocean.

Stand at the center of the Four Hidden Ways, where all Directions come together as One, at the sacred marker stone: Sense, See, and Feel, the Hidden Ways of East, South, North, and West. Let your mind pass along them in all directions to the very ends of the human world and the beginnings of the real world that lies beyond. Here is where all journeys begin and all journeys end: here, at the Crossroads.

Know this: the Crossroads is also a meeting place where many beings from different orders of life come together in equality and grace. It is our intention to meet with those Allies, Cousins, Co-Walkers and Spiritual Creatures, that are apt and willing to work with us in the task of redeeming the Surface World, bringing it closer and in harmony with the Primal World.

Be aware that they draw close, coming from the East, South, North and West. Some also rise up from the living Land Beneath, at the center of the Crossroads. They draw close, to meet us where the Four Hidden Ways come together, at the center of all Directions.

(Music)

Be aware that you are at the Crossroads, in the presence of your Allies, Cousins, Co-Walkers and Companion Spiritual Creatures. You may return here always, in your dreams, visions, meditations, and waking consciousness. They draw close to you, embrace you, and commune with you. Join with them now in silence.

(Short silent communion)

Be aware that out of the Host that has gathered, certain beings come to you, apt and fitting to work with you. You do not choose them, they come to you.

Sense, see, and feel these beings, and form clearly in your mind that your intention is to work with them in the art and discipline of the Spirit Cord. Let all your thought rest upon this one task, and vow to undertake it to the utmost of your ability.

Lift up your cord, holding the ends, right and left. Offer it up with outstretched arms. Do this physically, but also sense see and feel it in the spirit world, at the Crossroads, with the allies and spiritual creatures.

Hold the Cord up for as long as is needful. Sense, see and feel how they work with it.

Be still, keeping your arms up with the Cord, and commune in silence.

(Short silent communion)

Now you may sit with the Cord in your lap for a few moments, holding to your presence and communion at the Crossroads. Rest at this sacred Crossroads place and be at peace.

Now the Host begins to depart, and only your Close Companions remain. Declare to each of them that you will remember, realize, and return. They will each affirm their bond with you in their own manner.

Now open your eyes so that you are at the Crossroads but also aware of the outer world, wherever you may be. Rest upon the awareness that the Crossroads and your place in the outer world are one and the same, intertwined and inseparable.

Now be aware again of the Sky Above, the Land Below, and the Four Directions of the outer world. Be aware of what is in those Directions, be it city, oceans, open land, whatever is there, form it in your mind, see it, sense it, and feel it all about you.

As you return to the outer world, offer your thanks and respects to those Close Companions that have formed relationships with you. Acknowledge them to each of the Four Directions, and to the Land Below. Gradually their presence fades, and your presence in the human world increases.

Know that you may come and go freely, by way of the Crossroads, when you will. The Four Hidden Ways are open to you and the Mysteries of the Directions will be revealed to you as you travel the Hidden Ways. But for now, return to your human outer life. You have a direction behind you, a direction before you and directions to your right and left. And so you know your place, your way, and your potential.

With us is the Grace of the Shining Ones in the Mystery of Earth Light. Peace to all Signs and Shadows, Radiant Light to all Ways of Darkness, and the Living One of Light, Secret Unknown, Forever.

This concludes the Crossroad Form, offering up the Cord and empowering it through communion with the faery allies and spiritual creatures.

You may keep a journal and write notes if you wish. The deeper stages of this work, however, should not be written down as they must live in your memory rather than as details on paper. We will return to this theme of living memory again as it is essential in our context of Cord magic and spiritual practice.

Now we move on to the next initiatory form: *The Temple of Dedication.*

Chapter 8:
THE TEMPLE OF DEDICATION

Exploring People, Places and Powers

1. Images Time and Interaction (1)
2. Seeding Consciousness
3. OverWorld and UnderWorld
4. Where is the Temple of Dedication?
5. Place and Consciousness
6. The Potentials and Problems of Cultural Images
7. Images Time and Interaction (2)
8. Images and Archetypes
9. Images and Deities
10. Visualization and Empowered Vision
11. Entering the Temple of Dedication
12. Astral Double Dedication

IMAGES, TIME AND INTERACTION

In *The Temple of Dedication* form, we will be working with the spiritual allies and companions discovered at the Crossroads, the traditional faery and creature allies. However, we will be moving, in communion with them, to a deeper level. This form should be only done after you have performed the Crossroads form several times.

Without the experience and the Cord power of the Crossroads, this form will not work effectively for you. With the Cord power from the allies at the Crossroads as a foundation, this form will work strongly for you.

The Temple of Dedication is where the OverWorld and UnderWorld spiritual forces meet together. Thus it is of special significance for us, as humans, who stand between those two worlds or realms of consciousness. Before proceeding to the practical work, there are some helpful definitions, explorations and concepts that we should consider. You may pursue your cord work without these concepts, of course, but reading, thinking, and seeding them into your consciousness will substantially improve the subtle transmission and transformation that arises in the Temple of Dedication.

SEEDING CONSCIOUSNESS

The ubiquitous Tree of Life (Figure 8) shows how ideas and feelings (8th and 7th spheres, Mercury/Mind, and Venus/Emotion), when seeded deep into the individual consciousness, lead to stimulation and fertilization of the imagination (9th and 1st spheres, Moon/Foundation and Crown), and on to spiritual harmonic transformation (6th sphere, Sun/Beauty). This process is intentionally harnessed by our inner plane mentors, contacts, and transhuman Priests and Priestesses in their work with us. Concepts and feelings are planted like seeds in order that they may grow and be the vehicles for deeper consciousness. In group work a similar process occurs, often known as *induction*, whereby a talk about the techniques, concepts and traditions that are embodied within a ritual, visualization or meditation creates a field of consciousness in the room which enhances the group work considerably.

OVERWORLD AND UNDERWORLD

The terms OverWorld and UnderWorld are used in specific ways in this book, hence the atypical capitalization. I am aware that this

THE TEMPLE OF DEDICATION   93

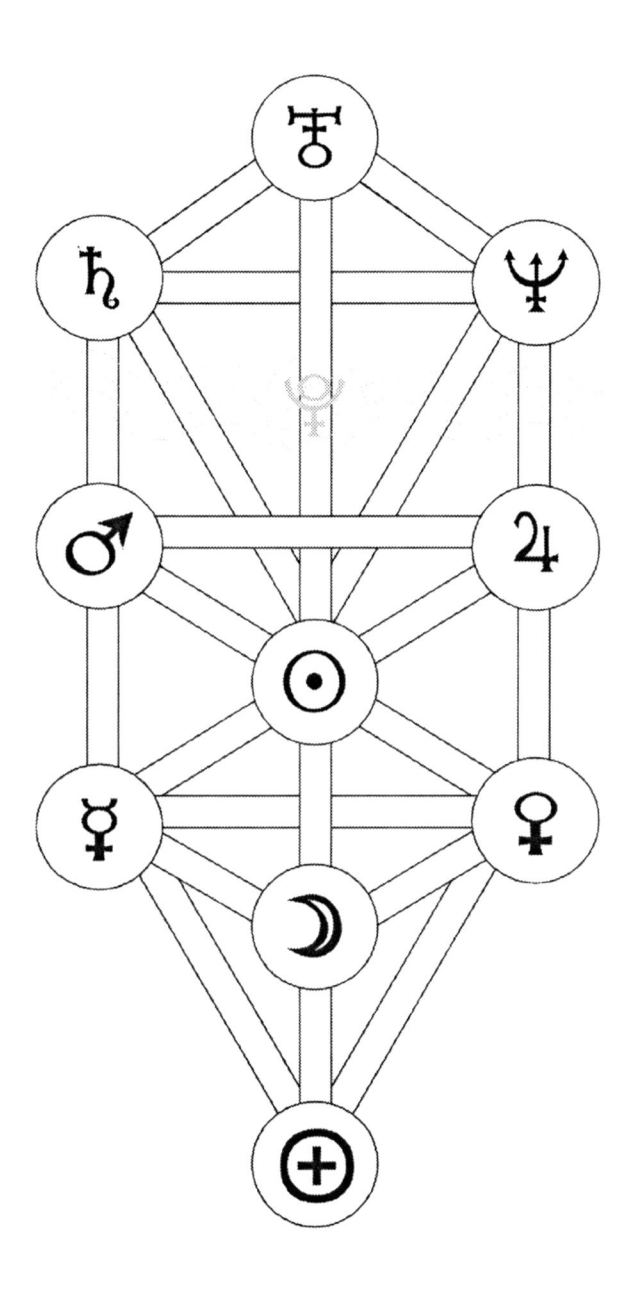

Figure 8

may create a somewhat anachronistic style, but it is not intended to be quaint. Its intent is to give us some simple terminology that avoids lengthy description whenever it is used. So here are the basic definitions that will be used, identified by their spelling throughout our text.

OverWorld means anything "off planet" such as the spiritual forces of the Moon, Sun and Planets, and Stars. This has long been regarded as the OverWorld due to the nature of our lives as beings within the gravity well of our planet. It creates the relativistic idea of "above."

> *In truth, both physically and metaphysically, there is no overworld, only an enfolding or around-world.*

The OverWorld, often thought of as "higher," enfolds our planet. By far the greatest proportion of the OverWorld is not above at all, but is on the horizons, in the four planetary directions, and beneath. Once we think of the OverWorld as being the off-planet sphere of influence of the Solar System, with its further cosmic presence in the holism or sphere of the Stellar world, we can begin to free up from the pernicious trap of dualism and the much repeated divisive nonsense derived from religious propaganda about "higher" planes.

Musical overtones or harmonics are sometimes cited as examples of higher patterns of being. Indeed, this model was well known in the ancient cultures and is central to the metaphysics found in works written by, or ascribed to, Plato and Pythagoras. Yet overtones, or higher octaves, are not linear or vertical, like the cosmos itself. They emanate in waves in a spherical expansion and contraction, assuming that there is no muting or blocking factor, such as a large overstuffed couch or an evolving star system. When we think of "above" or "higher," we must conceive of it as a small sector or segment of an encompassing field. Its context is within a sphere of spatial and metaphysical dimensions, never as a straight up and down line that demarcates conditions superior from conditions inferior.

UnderWorld means anything "in planet" such as the spiritual forces of the land, the ocean, and the deeper realms of energy and consciousness leading to and emanating from the planetary core. Thus the UnderWorld includes, but is not limited to, the faery realm, collective ancestral land-consciousness (which is deep at the foundations of all traditional or ancient magic and meta-physics), the realm of the greater consciousnesses, the large spiritual entities of land and ocean which were traditionally described as Titans or Giants, and many of the older gods and goddesses from pagan tradition. Most valuable for us, however, is the practical transformation that occurs when we intentionally and systematically move our awareness *into* the body of the land and planet, rather than off-planet in the often spurious and enervating "higher plane" meditations that dominate popular spirituality.

In truth, both physically and metaphysically, there is no underworld, only a within-world.

There is, however, a curious spiritual phenomenon that occurs when we change our direction of consciousness and move it away from the habitual outwardly-focused patterns of daily living in the consensual or "real" world. That is the world of extreme delusion and manipulation. When we go within, turning our awareness inwards in meditation or empowered vision, we eventually come to the stars. This stellar awareness may be found in both OverWorld and UnderWorld spiritual work, but the nearest sun power, the nearest star, is just beneath our feet, radiant in the core of planet Earth.

Thus, in our Cord work we do not use over- and underworld in a dualistic sense. Instead, they refer to interacting relativistic dimensions or states of being, of consciousness and energy. These states are defined both physically and metaphysically. This way of relating to over and under-worlds greatly clarifies and simplifies the spiritual life, and intentionally deflates the pernicious divisive nonsense about "higher planes" that permeates contemporary spiritual teachings, publications and popular thinking.

Divisive dualism in the modernist world is, of course, the direct result of Christian conditioning and suppression of awareness, along with that of Islam and Judaism. It has its origins in earlier religions and philosophies and is not solely the product of the Book religions. They received many aspects of divisive dualism from earlier religions and cultures, as dualism is a consciousness-trap that is inherent in humanity. Rather than waste endless hours discussing why this is so, the magician or esoteric student reaches into the deeper consciousness that is *before* dualism. From this altered perspective, we not only grow free of the trap, but we come to understand its true nature. To follow a spiritual path, to grow free of dualism, ignorance and self-indulgence, we must have dedication. This dedication can be strengthened, nourished and substantially assisted in its focus through the cord practices that we will undertake in the Temple of Dedication.

WHERE IS THE TEMPLE OF DEDICATION?

The Temple of Dedication is where the spiritual forces of Moon, Sun and Planets, and Stars meet with those of planet Earth. It is a threshold place and, in the context of our Cord work, it is where the consciousness of the inhabitants of Earth first touches, communes with, and receives the consciousness of the OverWorld. The key to understanding the significance of this threshold place is that the Temple of Dedication is, in an abstract sense, the state of consciousness that we enter while remaining on Earth, when we become *intentionally* aware of the off-planet forces of the OverWorld.

Such OverWorld or off-planet forces are those of the Solar System and Stars, personified from ancient times in many spiritual traditions as deities, planetary spirits, angels and archangels. In simple human terms we could by-pass the traditional vocabulary and think of these thresholds as being thresholds of consciousness. However, the traditional vocabulary is very useful to us providing that we can pass beyond its cultural inhibitions and contexts. It is useful because, at its core, it embodies a perennial and cross-cultural wisdom tradition that gives us many insights, maps and descriptions that help us find our way in the spiritual dimensions. Nor should we forget that this process of intentional awareness is not merely psychological or limited to the narrow space of the human brain or human personality. It involves interaction with other beings, ranging from those of the natural world on Earth, to those metaphysical entities that we encounter in our spiritual awareness, many of which have associated traditions of working with humanity.

Consider this: we are within the field of vast and complex OverWorld forces, continuously modified by that of Earth. We would have no existence without the interaction of these forces, both planetary and extra-planetary. But our awareness of them is almost entirely *unconscious*. It is our intention to be conscious, combined with the magical power of a chosen place (the Temple), that makes a substantial difference. The Temple of Dedication is where we open to a greater consciousness and discover ourselves to be a part thereof.

PLACE AND CONSCIOUSNESS

One of the most helpful and powerful laws of all magical or spiritual endeavor is this: *A state of consciousness is a Place: a place is a State of Consciousness.*

Do you doubt this? Think of how it applies in a daily outer sense to any city, region, country, forest, house, rocky slope, grassy plain, river, ocean or island. Is there anyone out there who will assert that Manhattan is *not* a state of consciousness or that peace of mind is *not* a place?

The qualities and interconnections of place and power (location and consciousness) become of vital importance in the inner or metaphysical worlds. When we move our awareness within, that which we customarily call an *inner temple* is simultaneously a place and a state of consciousness. It is created and held together by those beings, human and other, that populate it, by the subtle forces of the place itself, and by the powers that flow through it. In different cultures the imagery of an inner temple will vary. It may show as a Greek or Egyptian temple, a Hindu *ghat*, a location in the wilderness, a stone circle, or a Gothic Cathedral … but the inner power and purpose will remain the same. No matter what the presentation of the inner vision, the power and purpose of an inner temple, such as the Temple of Dedication, remains constant.

To open out this example further, let us consider as an example an inner temple of the intellect, of the arts and sciences. It might be seen with the inner vision or felt with the subtle senses as a modern complex of technology, or as a temple of Minerva or Athena, or of the Lord Ganesha. It can be seen as a stimulating clean pure high plateau with far reaching views or as the comprehensive library of a temple or monastery. They are all cultural or natural variants of the same *power* and *place* populated by a variety of *people* or spiritual beings. The visionary or outer form of such a temple will vary, but the temple itself remains unchanging at an energetic and functional level. In other words, the deeper power of the place will generate a variety of presentations, yet all will remain true to its own nature.

Within such varied presentations of inner temples, many people may enter and work together. Indeed, in our example of a temple of the intellect, arts and sciences, someone from a Hindu tradition may be in his or her cultural form of the Temple while someone else may be in a vast library and another on the high plateau – yet they are all in the same inner temple and all are working with the same spiritual forces that inspire intellect, music, arts, sciences, healing. Most important of all, they are working with one another, perhaps unaware, sometimes fully aware. This is how the magical arts work to bring the deeper cosmic forces through into manifestation. A sports man or woman might say that we are on several teams (often more than we know at first), but that we are all contributing together to the multiple team effort.

Thus there are several ways of embodying the metaphysical place/state which we call the Temple of Dedication. For practical purposes we will be using imagery enshrined within tradition that is relatively free of cultural attributes.

THE POTENTIALS AND PROBLEMS OF CULTURAL IMAGES

As a rule it is not always helpful to use culturally or historically specific images of temples or deities, as this requires that we enter a historical or cultural stream of tradition and living consciousness, and therefore we must be willing carry its burden. Consequently, we would not necessarily look for a Greek or Chinese historical manifestation of the inner temple, as this would limit our experience to a cultural ambience and collective psychic inheritance. We can work instead with the core concepts of the temple and embody it in primal imagery that is not limited to any one culture or tradition and yet will have a validity and resonance for many. Just behind and within the cultural imagery, there is a pan-cultural level that can be employed with great effect. This is what the magician priest or priestess engaged in sacro-magical tasks always seeks even when he or she begins with the cultural, the national, or the ethnic foundations. Thus we use the cultural themes and traditions, but are not limited to them or by them. We acknowledge their power and work with it, but we are not devotees or religionists.

Contemporary use of traditional source material is extremely powerful for us as it carries considerable weight from the collective consciousness. In this context we must think of and learn from the collective traditions that are at the foundation of magic, and which are woven into the foundations of even the most dogmatic religions. Furthermore, tradition is, of itself, an "alphabet" of magic which can be creatively formed into "words" and eventually into "spells" ... that is, into combinations of units as a complex interactive sequence. This is of such significance that it is worth restating.

IMAGES, TIME AND INTERACTION

Traditional imagery is the foundation, the alphabet, of magic. Such "images" are far from being a confused symbolic inheritance awaiting systematic interpretation and collation, as is arrogantly assumed in materialist psychology. Nor are they an outmoded or archaic set that has no validity in the modern world, for *without traditional images we would have no world at all.*

What is called traditional imagery, in this context, is the

foundation of consciousness that leads to manifestation. Thus it will always seem to be "of the past" because it speaks of a phase *before* the present one, yet it embodies and presents the very forces that enabled this "present" to come into shape. History has an illusion of linear progression: the idea that this event leads to that event. Yet, the shaping forces are preserved and encapsulated in sets of images. Some of these sets have been formalized as deities or legends. Others are found within widespread myths concerning the nature of existence, while specialist sets are found in esoteric traditions, magical arts and so forth. These images are held in the collective memory, sometimes loosely called the racial unconscious, an area of planetary ancestral and collective consciousness. It has been undergoing major disruption and change during our time since at least the early 20th century, and is increasing in acceleration during this 21st century. Prior the early 20th century, there was a racial and cultural continuity among humans, and an integral continuity among ecosystems and species in nature, that had held for many centuries. Today no one would deny the disruption, discontinuity and change. Our human perspective is too short for us to truly evaluate such changes, though we are most aware of the dramatic effects that we dislike or for which we know that humanity is responsible.

In Cord work, we can assist harmoniously in such changes and work to redeem imbalances when in the Temple of Dedication.

IMAGES AND ARCHETYPES

The idea of "archetypes" as employed in Jungian and post-Jungian psychology is loosely derived from this substantially older concept of enduring sets of images found in the wisdom traditions and philosophy of the ancient world, and in magical and spiritual arts. But we must be cautious in our acceptance, as the so-called *archetypes* of contemporary popular psychology are merely a sub-set, or therapeutic definition list, artificially formulated for limited purposes in this materialist age. The word *archetype* originally meant something very different from the general usage today, as it is a Greek word describing cosmic universal matrices. It is by no means limited to the current widely used and popularized images of the human psyche. A classic dictionary definition is:

An original model or type after which other similar things are patterned; a prototype: [Latin archetypum, from Greek arkhetupon, from neuter of arkhetupos, original: arkhe-, arkhi- , archi- + tupos, model, stamp.]

The problem with the artificial re-definition of the word archetype in psychology (if it is a problem) lies with the bland assumption that there is nothing outside the human psyche. This implies that the vast resources of traditional imagery and perennial wisdom are actually the product of a pre-psychological ignorance, straining unsuccessfully towards that which was only discovered by Freud, Jung, Adler, et al. This pernicious notion was originated by C.G. Jung, who borrowed freely from the magical perennial traditions. It was then repeatedly asserted that he had liberated this material into a scientific form. This stance taken by Jung in his works is not only pretentious but woefully inadequate, no matter how effective it may have been for loosening up the straight-laced European middle-classes a hundred years past.

The image-sets of the human psyche, which are sub-sets of cosmic archetypes, are far from being a secret discovered by the pioneers of therapy in 19th century Europe. They have been widely known, taught, explored and employed for thousands of years worldwide. All spiritual and magical traditions have their own branches of psychology. When we ignore the claims of materialist psychology and explore the older traditions themselves, we find profound psychological insight and many traditional methods for individual liberation, harmonious inner integration, and inner transformation. Furthermore, there is a perennial and embracing continuity and connection between all such magical/spiritual psychologies in all traditions. They offer different cultural presentations of the same truths.

What is of considerable significance for us is that the image-set of the human psyche, with primal units such as Mother, Rival, Eternal Child, and many more, is *not* the entire human consciousness. It is merely that fragment which develops to operate within any one human culture in any one lifetime. We are much more, and we can be consciously aware of much more. This is the core difference between a materialist psychology and a spiritual psychology.

To summarize: the human psyche as it is described in modern materialist psychology is not all that we are. The old Hermetic wisdom teaching, found in many spiritual traditions, states that *All is Mind* is true, but that Mind is the cosmic mind. It is not merely the ephemeral human psyche that is contained with the cosmic mind.

Nor is our own awareness limited to that which occurs within the psyche. Many of the forces, forms and processes that we experience are not within our individual consciousness, but have an independent existence. This other zone of existence is traditionally called the spirit world. It is in this world, this complex of metaphysical dimensions, that the images preserved in tradition speak to us and may be heard by us, and wherein we may interact with them.

To offer an example: we can easily accept that an average human has, within the consciousness, personality and psyche, an image of his/her mother, as a primal image deriving from birth and childhood. It need not be solely applied to the birth mother, but to any and every person or thing exhibiting qualities of motherliness that trigger a response from the individual concerned. The responses and guiding impulses from within may be recognized consciously, or they may be unconscious. Thus far, the psychological model of the so-called archetype holds true and good, and can be helpful both in therapy and within a limited self-understanding that is beginning to reflect upon itself and gain insights.

However, the traditional images work in a different way. The image of the mother may connect to that of a mother goddess. This is the type of example beloved of those psychologists who try to lay claim to the spiritual and magical traditions, supposedly bringing them out of their pre-psychological ignorance into the light of scientific reason. But the goddess is a spiritual power *outside* the individual with a link or conduit to the psyche through the embedded mother image of childhood. When we work consciously, we discover that each of the varied goddess images from spiritual or magical traditions bring different forces into our lives. This is where the old idea of "attributes" comes from. The deities, supernatural entities and spiritual allies are not the archetypes claimed by psychology. They are other independent entities with their own volition. They can, and often do, link into the deep cultural or familial images within the individual (those same images that are incorrectly called "archetypes"). Until we realize this truth, the psychological approach is little more than a method of reductionism and, at its worse, a posture of clever systematization. Once we have realized this truth concerning archetypes and entities, images and consciousness and explored it in practical meditational and spiritual experience, the modern psychological approach (stripped of its propaganda and inflated claims) can find a useful place within an overall perspective of human consciousness. Indeed, given the pervasive influence of psychology in modern culture, it is often necessary nowadays simply in order to find ways to be free of it. But it is not essential to undergo therapy before entering on a spiritual path. The path, any spiritual path, provides the therapy and transformation rapidly and effectively if we stay upon it. How could it not? Any spiritual path is a path of transformation.

IMAGES AND DEITIES

If you *worship* the deities, you personify them. If you *work* with them respectfully without subservience or superstition, you come to understand that they embody a wide range of forces, each according to attributes known in tradition. But in both cases, that of worship and that of intentional spiritual work, it is the image, established in tradition (be it Buddhist, pagan, Christian, Native American, Celtic, Norse, Hindu, Chinese, or whatever), that acts as a gateway for the spiritual power to pass through. In neither case is this portal image limited to the human psyche alone.

Gods and goddesses are not the only People contained within the traditional storehouse of images, for there are many others. Such

People inhabit Places, and these Places are also handed down as images in tradition. Such images are found to have coherence worldwide, albeit with many cultural differences. This is not because they embody shared psychological "archetypes," but because they describe states and places of consciousness and energy that are beyond, but freely accessible to, the human psyche.

When we take the images and concepts of tradition, work with them and shape them into coherent forms for contemporary use, we are involved in true living spiritual magic.

Visualization and Empowered Vision

For some years it has been customary, even dogmatically demanded, to include lengthy written texts of visualization in books on magic and spirituality. As a general rule these will work if they come from inspired inner contact and genuine vision, though quality of the text itself is important. Conversely such screeds will often fail to work, not just because they may be poorly written, but because they are contrived, artificial and therefore lifeless. Many writers assume that if you follow some basic templates and create a text-based visualization following a chosen theme, then that is it … it has to work. Often the task of *assembling a text* is mistaken for the task of *opening out a visualization* that will resonate for others. They are not the same.

Text-based visualization has to come from the inner consciousness, not from the keyboard and the spell-checker. If the writer has not had the vision first, if the writer has not created the text out of that vision rather than trying to create the vision from the text, then the text is sterile in the sense that it cannot give birth to anything.

In practice, less is more. Pages and pages of descriptive text tend to bore and distract the reader and are extremely difficult, in practice, to use for visualization or meditation. Many people like the comfort factor of a defined text. But sometimes lengthy content becomes a substitute for actual practice. In essence it is possible to create an empowered vision, which is a visionary scenario with inherent spiritual forces and active inner contacts, with a small amount of text. To demonstrate this method, we will explore the scenario for the Temple of Dedication and discover the inner workings of this short empowered vision. Such work begins with a simple direct scenario and subsequently develops through several stages, all of which are described in our empowered vision or form. Then, of course, you should proceed to work in the Temple itself!

ENTERING THE TEMPLE OF DEDICATION

The basic components of this form are found within the hallowed *landscape method* of traditional magic. Many myths, legends, folk and faery tales work within a sacred living landscape in which the powers ascribed to the directions (East, South, North and West) create a theater-of-consciousness within which all action takes place. Little wonder this was so significant in the ancestral consciousness: everything that we are and all that we do is embodied and enabled within the planetary directions. Without them, we could not exist. Therefore, when we work magic, we always seek to work consciously with the directions. Once again, we must remember that *participation* is everything. This is how the theater of the sacred directions works, just as our life within the planetary directions works. Indeed, both sets of directions, the sacred and the mundane, are aspects of one another and may not be artificially separated.

It is of great significance that we live in a time and culture wherein very few people have any idea of their ongoing relationship to the planetary directions. While we might have general ideas of the directions for travel by car or plane, many people have no inherent sense of the directions in their home place or work place. Many cannot tell where the sun or moon rises in relationship to their homes. This is not surprising, for we are a people that have lost context. Context has been replaced by media entertainment, which becomes a pseudo-context, a daily rhythm, a sole source of conversation and direction. The Sun has become, for us, the television in the lounge and is no longer the radiant star that gives life to all beings on Earth.

The Mountain of the North

The Temple of Dedication is on the mountain of the North. The mountain of the North is a dormant volcano and the temple is in the crater at the summit. The temple is sensed as a stone structure, usually of megalithic type such as a large chamber made of massive stones, fitted together without mortar. In the center is the Altar of Dedication, which is a large circular flat stone altar made from one single slab.

When activated through our inner senses, this simple scenario can lead us into communion with potent spiritual forces and with spirit beings apt and fitting for our tasks; those that are accustomed to working harmoniously with humans. Such spiritual powers and people empower our cords, weaving into them the subtle energies and lines of connection that are needful. Working with a few sparse images of a real inner temple is considerably more powerful than laboring over substantial pages of descriptive text of a fantasy. Let us unpack our summary of the empowered vision of the Temple of Dedication, step by step, and consider what is contained within these few sentences above:

1. *The Direction North of the sacred landscape.* North is associated with transformation, death and eventual rebirth. It is the direction of Wisdom, of the Element of Earth, and of the Dark Mother Goddess. North is also the direction of midnight stars whereby stellar forces are received directly by the planet Earth, without influence of Sun or Moon. There are further subtle associations with Grace and Peace in the North, as well as that timeless time that we experience between death and rebirth. In ancient tradition, North was the place of the Sacred Stone, the power of spirit utterly present in substance.

2. *The Sacred Mountain.* The Mountain is found in all spiritual traditions, in varying forms, as the place of climbing to the stars and reaching towards the off-planet spiritual forces. This concept is familiar in popular spirituality and meditation but, like the mountain

itself, there is much more to be explored underneath than is visible and obvious on the surface.

The Sacred Mountain, in any spiritual tradition, is not a path of escape. Spiritual practices on mountains are about climbing to a place where the OverWorld may be contacted, clear of the influences of the lowlands, both geographically and within one's self. What is usually forgotten, or more typically unknown, is that the energy that shaped the mountain comes from the UnderWorld. This is true both physically and spiritually. When we are on the mountain, we are supported by vast planetary forces, those telluric powers that uplift both the mountain and ourselves towards Moon, Sun and Stars. The Sacred Mountain is alive: its roots extend down into the fiery heart of the Earth. Volcanic, telluric and geomantic forces flow through the mountain, even though its crater is currently dormant. Thus the mountain uplifts us towards the stars, but also holds the way open for the Earth Light, that spiritual power which ascends from the planetary core of energy and consciousness.

In traditional imagery, the mountain is described as being hollow. Inside the mountain are various halls and chambers. In the faery and UnderWorld traditions these take specific forms with well-defined functions and inhabitants. Once again, we should remember that this way of working with consciousness (of interaction within a scenario that has inhabitants) is not a fantasy. Using the scenario as a gateway enables us to come into contact with real and active forces, with independent metaphysical entities, and to undergo spiritual transformations. The key is always that the scenario is enshrined within tradition, rather than a fantasy or artificial textual construct.

As we progress with our Cord work, we will discover and experience ways of communing with the various metaphysical People and Powers that occupy the Mountain. Like all Mysteries, the Sacred Mountain combines Place, People and Power.

Let us proceed now to our major form and our spiritual work within the Temple of Dedication

The Temple of Dedication

The Temple of Dedication is on the mountain of the North. The mountain of the North is a dormant volcano and the temple is in the crater at the summit. The temple is sensed, seen, and felt, as a stone structure, usually of megalithic type such as a large chamber made of massive stones, fitted together without mortar. In the center is the Altar of Dedication, which is a large circular flat stone altar made from one single slab.

Note: For this form, your cord should be around the back of your neck with the ends held in the right and left hands.

Be still, stilling Time, Space and Movement.

(Light your altar flame, if possible.)

Build strongly with your inner vision the image of the Sacred Mountain. See, sense and feel the Sacred Mountain before you. You intend to go to it. With this intention, the image of the mountain expands and grows and you move towards it at speed.

Now you find yourself on the mountain top. There is a large crater and you are within it seeing the clouds streaming in the sky above its rock walls. In the centre of the crater is the temple made of huge natural rocks laid close together. You intend to enter this chamber and you pass within.

The interior is shadowy and calm. There is a circular stone altar with a radiant flame burning upon it.

Draw close and be still, stilling Time, Space and Movement.

(Pause for stillness)

Now raise the ends of your cord towards the flame *(do this also in the outer world with your physical cord)*. Sense, see and feel that a mirror image of your cord appears on the altar. Just as your cord is around your neck, so its astral double is around the flame.

The flame on the Altar of Dedication expands and grows becoming a pillar of light extending to the height of the stars and descending to the depths of the UnderWorld. The astral double of your cord joins with your physical cord, making a complete link between your body and the Pillar of Light.

Here and now make your vow. Be it great or small, declare your intention and commitment. As you do so, mighty spirit beings arise from the mountain beneath to bear witness, to support and to strengthen you.

Commune now in silence. As you do so, spiritual beings descend from above to commune with you. Feel the subtle forces flow in and out of your cord, and your body.

(Silent communion)

Know that you are in the Temple of Dedication, in the crater on the summit of the Sacred Mountain. You are in the presence of the Mighty Ones of Earth and Stars. Know that you may return here in your dreams, visions and meditations.

This sacred place hallowed for many thousands of years is a resource for you. Come here to make your vow and to draw strength and inspiration for its fulfilment.

Be aware again of the Pillar of Light. See, sense and feel it fade into a single flame. The presence of the Mighty Ones recedes. Discover that the flame upon the altar is also the flame of being within you, at the centre of the directions. Now return to your outer awareness sensing the sky above, the land below, and the four directions of East, South, West and North.

Take the cord from your neck and thus close your working in the Temple of Dedication.

(If you lit a candle, extinguish it. Your cord can go on the altar around the candle. If you are working without altar and candle, the cord should go into its bag.)

Astral Double Dedication

Here is what you do, in this case step-by-step without the dramatic induction narrative used above.

1. With your physical Cord that has first been empowered at the Crossroads of the Faery Realm, the Ancestors and the UnderWorld, go to the Temple of Dedication.

You should always enhance this process by doing some physical action with the Cord (working both with the Cord and your body). At the least this should be done by holding the cord when you work to enter the Temple. Remember to practice the Cord Positions described in Chapter 5.

2. Place the Cord around the back of your neck with the right and left ends in your hands.

3. Extend the Cord towards the Altar of Dedication so that your hands and the ends of the Cord are on the altar.

4. The double of your Cord will appear to your inner senses either visually, or tangibly, or both. While your physical cord is around the back of your neck, the double is around the Pillar of Light in the centre of the altar. The ends of the double merge with the ends of your physical cord.

You can enhance this method by using a simple altar with a candle and making the outer movements match and merge with the inner presence.

5. Commune in silence. You will feel something flowing between the astral cord and the physical. You may also feel this flowing within your body. If this sense of energy flowing within the body occurs, do not use popular techniques concerning the "chakras," but remain still and at peace, allowing the subtle forces to circulate spontaneously. If you try to steer them you will break the connection.

As a general rule it is good to ignore any popular teachings on energy or chakras when you do Cord work as they will disrupt or inhibit the flow of subtle forces. With practice you will grow beyond these popular techniques and move into a new arena of spiritual energetics.

6. Make any dedication, vow or request at this stage. And again, be still.

7. Withdraw from the Temple of Dedication, affirm the Directions of the outer world: East, South, West, North, Sky Above, and Land Below. Gently extinguish the candle. Take the cord from your neck and place it on your altar, or in its back.

You can write notes at this stage if you wish, but it is preferable to hold the experiences in living memory and gradually move away from note taking and journaling.

In our next chapter, we move through the mysterious threshold between the Earth and OverWorld, and enter into the Lunar Realm.

CHAPTER 9:
THE LUNAR REALM

*The Gold and Silver Stairs
and the Lunar Archangel*

1. Interaction with the Sub-Lunar World
2. How Far Can You Go?
3. The Long Way, the Short Way
4. Nothing in Between?
5. Expansion of Awareness
6. The Gold and Silver Stairs
7. Understanding the Lunar Archangel
8. The Cord, the Archangel, and the World

INTERACTION WITHIN THE SUB-LUNAR WORLD

In this form we use an original empowered vision which is broadly based upon a traditional method and set of images found within western mysticism and Qabalistic tradition. The aim of this form, as with all our Cord Forms, is to weave, into your physical cord, specific spiritual forces and communion with certain inner contacts. Gradually the cord embraces and comes to embody a comprehensive and ongoing set or holism, an open-ended interlacement, of spiritual forces and contacts. This interlacement does not close or complete. If it were to be completed it could only decay. It is open-ended because it transcends time, space and movement, and has the potential to link to all aspects of the cosmos through the matrices that we traditionally call the three worlds of Moon, Sun and Stars. This may seem like a vast project, but in practice it opens out simply, step by step, and works directly through the inherent nature of the Cord on all levels, physical to spiritual, manifest to transcendent. All you need is a piece of string.

The sacro-magical aspects of cord embodiment are the unique core of our work and of this book. As a result of the methods taught herein, the physical cord, with its interwoven contacts, is ultimately attuned to the astral double of the cord which energises the physical cord throughout your life, or in the case of more than one life, the physical *cords* with which we work. Cord work is ongoing, providing continuity between lives. In practice we find that many, though not all, people drawn to this work feel that they have "done it before." This feeling may be due to previous cord work in other lives but is ultimately founded upon the spiritual nature of the Cord whereby it connects our spiritual awareness to our outer or habitual consciousness. This connection is not bound by time, so the sense of doing Cord work before is really a deep comprehension that the cord exists as a cosmic theme of connection. Do not be disappointed, however, if you feel that you have never done any Cord work before: what is valuable is that you commit to doing it and then continue to do it rather than merely gain an inventory of whether-or-not you have done it before!

We can use a poetic analogy to describe the inner or spiritual nature of the cord: in most individuals the Cord of Spirit is coiled or even tangled around the body. Many of its knots and convolutions are emotional while some are shaped from forces brought through at birth. It is often difficult to reach past the knots towards that part of the Cord that extends and connects into the spiritual words and leads towards our true Being. By undertaking conscious Cord work, we untangle our Cord of Spirit and follow it to its mysterious Source.

The early stages of this work, which cannot be bypassed or ignored, require interaction with the sub-lunar world which is a realm of consciousness and energy that is especially sensitive to the power of the imagination that we employ during our lifetime. This is the realm in which the art of visualization is helpful.

As discussed in our previous chapters a "visualization," or empowered vision, should not be merely text-based, but must come from, and actively connect to, a genuine inner vision. In our cord work (as presented in this book and in classes and workshops), many of the forms are entirely original while some are new and unique versions based upon traditional practices, such as the Crossroads (Chapter 6).

The *Gold and Silver Stair* is an original presentation of a broadly defined method that has been employed for centuries, in various ways, by mystics and magicians. Our form embodies a precise and carefully attuned method of moving the awareness "off-planet" while keeping within the boundaries of the sub-lunar world.

While the Temple of Dedication (Chapter 7) is as far as we can reach and still be touching the Earth, the Gold and Silver Stair guides our feet off our mother Earth and out into the mysterious field of consciousness that surrounds the planet. This is the Foundation, or sub-lunar world described by the medieval and Renaissance magicians. It is of great significance and value for us in our practical cord work.

Magical work in the sub-lunar realm has been neglected due to the unhealthy emphasis upon a purely psychological approach to magic that arose in the 20th century. Part of our task, not only in our Cord work, but in the overall re-evaluation and restoration of magical arts for the 21st century, is to come into a strong relationship with the sub-lunar realm and to develop clear and effective techniques for working therein.

This task is important for a number of reasons. First, and most obvious, though most readily misunderstood, is that of our own individual spiritual growth and perception. Second, the sub-lunar realm holds the hidden keys to many mysteries of death and rebirth, sleep and waking, remembering and forgetting. Third, and of considerable import for humanity at this time, is that the sub-lunar realm generates the tides of oceans, of weather and of the rise and fall of species, health and disease, and destruction and regeneration of all life forms on earth. Not of life itself, but of the life forms, species and patterns, through which life manifests into form in Nature. More simply, the sub-lunar world holds the keys to the active redemption and rebalancing of our current environmental and health crises.

Once we have moved our awareness into this realm, we are gradually able to interact with its subtle forces especially the tidal energies that move into and out of manifestation flowing through all living beings and through the planet itself. Traditionally our interaction is enabled by a relationship with the angelic consciousness or the intelligences of the lunar sphere, known as *Aishiim*, from a Semitic root word meaning Flames. These intelligences or angels traverse the space between the Moon and the Earth, but are, in their nature, of the Moon more than of the Earth.

When we say "of the Moon" we are referring not only to the physical moon that scribes and defines the sphere containing Earth but to the vast spiritual dimension of the Foundation of the Universe which is embodied for us in this solar system as the interaction between our planet and its moon. This greater and lesser Foundation is sometimes a source of confusion for students as contemporary spirituality and psychology often offers, through ignorance, a trivialised set of definitions for that which is lunar (the dream world, the unconscious and so forth, all conceived of as being within the skull).

In esoteric tradition, the sub-lunar world enfolds and includes our Earth and Moon; they are really one entity. The holism of energies from this interactive relationship of Earth and Moon is the Foundation of all manifest being. This is our first, or microcosmic, understanding of the Foundation.

This microcosmic level of planet-moon interaction mirrors a greater interaction which is the Foundation of cosmic manifestation. More simply, it happens everywhere, but we are mostly concerned with our own neighbourhood.

The Aishiim, angelic beings of the Foundation and sub-lunar world, are often described in tradition as sources of softly shining silver radiance with no clearly defined shape. We will return to them shortly.

How Far Can You Go?

When we move our awareness off-planet (a procedure popularly called *rising through the planes*), how far can we go? While there are many theoretical descriptions and methods, most of which seem to create only an illusion of rising, usually combined with an immature rejection of the material world; a rejection that frequently arises from a sense of frustration and failure therein. To a certain extent, this rejection may be a useful starting point as it can lead to a further and deeper sense that the world is not as it seems. But if it is associated with an emotional knot or convolution in the individual cord, with a sense of failure or lack of self-worth, rising through the planes can lead to a monstrous inflation of the ego – a bolstering of the ephemeral self image that can so easily dominate and delude. In other words, such a fantasy of rising through the planes based upon text descriptions rather than actual experience, may under such circumstances, replace and effectively block any true movement of awareness. Unravelling the tangled cord, however, brings us into a true sense of self.

The Long Way, the Short Way

To return to our question of "how far?" the simple answer is this: either a long way or a short way but, for most people, nothing in between.

The long way is the goal of the mystic and as such we can achieve moments of profound union with the cosmos through meditation, going a long way from our habitual awareness of the outer manifest world on a lightning fast journey that reaches to the source of the stars. Such moments are usually brief: they correspond to the furthest point on the long journey that we take at death, travelling far, for a little while, beyond self-identity and consciousness before we return into a new life on Earth. Everyone goes out a long way when they die but this journey is soon forgotten.

The short way is that other journey that we all take when we sleep. We move out of the normal direction of consciousness into a realm that corresponds to the surrounding mantle of consciousness/ energy that is just off-planet and enfolds the entire Earth and every living creature the sub-lunar realm. This is, for us in normal sleep, the dream world, but it is not unreal or trivial, and most important, it is not limited to the small storehouse of the skull and brain. We return from this short journey upon waking. Just as we forget our furthest reach of spirit that occurs at death, so do we forget most of what happens during sleep.

Both the long journey and the short can be reproduced by special methods and training, in such a manner that they do not involve the usual processes of either death or sleep.

Methods are extremely varied ranging through many forms and traditions from complex ritual to abstract contemplation. Here, of course, we are working with Cord forms for taking the long or short journey in full awareness, and with full memory of the experience. That memory may fade from our mental checklist of what we think we know but it does not fade from the cord. *The cord remembers for us.*

Death and sleep are harmonics of one another and both are emitted from, and resonate with, another state of consciousness beyond manifestation or incarnation which is known to the inner or esoteric traditions and which can be realised within you in any one lifetime. We will return to this concept again, in several places in this book.

Nothing in Between?

The places in between sleep and death and between the short and long journeys into and out of manifest consciousness on Earth, are described in religious magical and mystical texts. But they are seldom experienced spontaneously. Everyone takes the short journey and the long journey but very few choose to go to the places in between. As discussed briefly above, there are many delusions associated with "rising through the planes" or "invoking higher powers" which are usually ego-inflating variants of escapism. This is not to imply that we may not rise through the planes or invoke higher consciousness ... of course we *may*, but this depends on whether or not we *can*.

The In Between places/states of consciousness are traditionally mapped upon the Tree of Life (Figure 8). It is extremely significant that this glyph shows that stages and states of consciousness are embodied within planetary forces ... or, to put it another way, our consciousness goes off-planet from Earth and encounters other modes of awareness as it goes *further out* into the spiritual forces of the Solar System. This is a very different proposition from the widely accepted notion that the planets "symbolise" qualities or drives within the human psyche. Such a psychological approach can greatly reduce and disempower magic, effectively imprisoning our awareness within a subtly materialist straight-jacket.

It also leads to the spiritual sickness of solipsism, in which the personality focuses upon itself as the source and sum of all things – of all that happens. This is the equivalent of a loop of tape or a loop of code replaying itself ceaselessly unconnected to anything else. Humans are more than this self-iterating personal aspect of the psyche and can, with effort and focus, dispose of it utterly. Indeed, we do dispose of it utterly each time we die. Nothing takes more effort and focus than death. The more practised we are at focussing awareness and clarifying imagination, the easier each death becomes, be it the little death of any life change over the years or the physical death at the closing of a lifetime on Earth.

EXPANSION OF AWARENESS

What is often called expansion of awareness, or rising through the planes, is the result of an individual consciousness moving off-planet and interacting with the spiritual forces of our Solar System. This may be done in several ways, through inward direction of meditation, through visionary work and through ritual. The deeper we go within, the further off-planet. The same holds true for entering the UnderWorld where we move the consciousness into the body of the Earth. This method, widely used in ancestral traditions, leads to a cosmic or stellar expansion of consciousness. What does not work so well is to merely fantasize rising through the planes according to a text book map.

Expansion of awareness is temporary ... limited by time. When we go into expanded awareness we lose our sense of time. When we come out of it, we regain our sense of time. What is really important and valuable in the spiritual life is not so much any *expansion* of awareness, which is often evanescent, but *transformation* of awareness which continues and fades not.

The greater entities which are manifest as the planets and moons of our solar system, embody for us on Earth certain cosmic forces. They hold, as tradition informs us, both planetary attributes and cosmic attributes simultaneously. This arises from the mirroring and imprinting of the astral light that is discussed in Chapter 4.

The traditional planetary forces of Neptune, Saturn, Jupiter, Mars Venus, Mercury, Moon and Earth are all solar expressions uttered by our sun of greater cosmic forces uttered by all stars. They are not symbols but entities that embody energy. The Sun is a Star. These cosmic energies, these utterances of consciousness/energy, are mirrored on Earth in the sub-lunar world and again in the human body and consciousness. The Tree of Life is a glyph or map that helps us to discover the relationship between the lesser and greater mirrorings, imprints and patterns that are manifest through the bodies: the human body; the Earth/Moon body; the planetary bodies and the body of the solar system (which is a stellar body).

The component planets, moons and satellites of our solar system are the body and organs of one entity, the solar Being. Its main organ, or heart, and source of being is our own star, the sun. Its entirety, its complete body, is the whole solar system. As humans we are within the field of consciousness and energy of the Foundation which is that sphere defined around Earth by the rapid orbits of the Moon. When we move our awareness out of this sphere, we come into the threshold sphere of the moon itself, of the sun and planets and of the stars. Each of these three, often termed the Three Worlds, mediates cosmic forces within the solar system in addition to radiating its own forces. This is as true physically as it is metaphysically. Our life on Earth is within a vast complex of radiated energies from the sun and planets which in turn modulate and mediate stellar forces. If we are to expand our awareness we must reach off-planet, not to escape to "higher realms," but to come into a conscious and defined relationship with, and an awareness of, those subtle intelligences *within which we already live.*

In spiritual arts awareness is often transformed by going within...we use the terms inner awareness and inner contacts freely in this kind of work. But this is not the narcissistic or solipsistic self-reference of the personality, or the ego of psychology. It is a going within that comes into the mirroring of the greater Being within the lesser being. By going within, we can reach beyond ourselves. This does not mean that off-planet awareness or rising through the planes is purely subjective, but that by reaching within we come into a transformed awareness that resonates with and attunes to the extra-planetary consciousness. Therefore we rise, we go off-planet. All magical and spiritual arts ultimately aim towards this transformation; this redefining of our relationship with the world in which we live. Thus we move from the personal world into a transpersonal world. On the way we change our relationship to planet Earth, and gradually come into new awareness of the Sun and Planets of our solar system. They are no longer merely the physical bodies that radiate and move, but are discovered to be sources of intelligence that are in harmony with one another, and which in a greater pattern mediate stellar or cosmic awareness.

Let us move on now, to the practical form for *Climbing the Stairs.*

THE GOLD AND SILVER STAIRS

Note: this Cord form is modular, in that you can add the successive parts once you have practiced. Thus, you would begin with Part 1 only, adding Part 2 when you have practiced 1, and so forth. It is not advisable to experiment with the later parts before training in the earlier stages of this work. The parts are:

(1) (1a), Ascending and Descending
(2) The Lunar Temple
(3) The Lunar Archangel and the Oceans

Part (1): Ascending and Descending

The Candle and the Door

Begin by lighting a candle. The flame is the Flame of Being that is at the heart of All.

Your Cord should be around the back of your neck (see Figure 1) for this working.

Be still, stilling time, space and movement.

Let your awareness rest on the flame: begin with eyes open.

The flame becomes a door of fire, with guardian beings on either side. You may proceed with eyes open or closed from this point.

On the other side of the door of fire is the gold and silver stair. Sense, see and feel this: a stairway with alternate gold and silver steps. It leads into a soft pearlescent mist, and climbs steeply upwards.

Be aware that you have traversed this stair, both up and down, many times. You descended it at birth, you ascended it at death. Each night as you cross into sleep you ascend this gold and silver stair, and when you awaken, you descend it into the manifest world.

Now are going to climb the gold and silver stair while in full waking consciousness. There are few who do so ... too few.

Climbing the Stair

Holding the ends of your Cord in your right and left hands, you pass through the door of fire. The guardian beings have many wings, many eyes, and each carries a sword of flame. By the virtue of your presence at the Crossroads and of the oath you have made in the Temple of Dedication, they allow you to pass and they guard the threshold for your safe return to the human world.

As you set your foot upon the stairs, invisible presences come to your right and left. You feel them like a breath of wind on either side. These are the angels and ministers of grace that attend you at death and at birth. Now, for the first time, you come into a waking relationship with them. Form a clear intention in your mind that you will come to know them well.

Uplifted on either side, you ascend the gold and silver stairs. At first you move slowly but gradually your speed increases. You pass through the veil of mist and become lighter, more mobile. You find yourself in a deep indigo hued space, vast and calm. Floating through this are many softly radiant lights. Occasionally one or more of these will move rapidly downwards or upwards.

Pause here, and sense see and feel the presence of these living flames in the sub-lunar realm. Especially feel them through your body: your body responds to them, and you know them in a wordless and deeply comprehensive way through your bones. Know that you can return here in your dreams visions and waking meditations.

Contemplation and Communion: be still, stilling time, space and movement. Be present in the sub-lunar realm.

Part (1a) Descending

Descending the Stair

Now you may return down the stairs. You may climb down slowly at first, as you would a ladder in the manifest world. Soon you will turn and face back to the world of nature, which you see sense and feel through the glowing mist below. Your angelic ministers support you, as you retrace the steps that you took at every birth.

Now you emerge back where you began your journey on the gold and silver stairs. Pause and consider the Flame of Being. Now extinguish the candle, take off your Cord, and return to the outer world.

End of Part 1

Part (2): The Lunar Temple

Begin this form with the cord in the half-open position, as shown in Figure 3.

NOTE: when you do this, do not use images of lunar gods or goddesses, or of formalised temple structures, as these will limit the potential of the experience. Let the Moon Temple be whatever it will, as your intent is to find it and pass within. It can take many forms and have many different aspects of divinity within. Do not limit, but allow to be.

Ascend the stair as in part (1)

Be aware that the streaming lights of the lunar angels flow in and out of the Earth, coming and going mysteriously. Try to sense see and feel their source, by being very still and sensing it through your entire body. After this stillness, build an image before you, in the lunar world, of the Moon Temple.

See sense and feel this temple, which may take several forms, and approach its entrance. It shines with a silver-white light that gives great clarity … and you feel it clarifying your own awareness and subtle forces.

Now you pass within the Moon Temple. Before you is a veil of radiant violet waves of light and your attendant ministers of grace part this veil and guide you through.

The sanctuary of the Moon Temple is empty but for a closed vessel or container upon the altar. Be still and contemplate this vessel. *(pause for silent meditation here)*

When the vessel opens, throw one end of your cord into it. *(Be sure to cast the physical cord in the outer world as you do this)*

Thus you are holding one end of the cord, and the other stretches out before you ... reaching into the vessel upon the altar in the Temple of the Moon.

Place your end of the cord upon the three central body zones in turn *(do not think of or try to work with chakras)*. There is a flow, a rhythm, to this threefold pattern: feel it. At each zone, pause and be still.

1. The navel or loins
2. The heart
3. The brow

Now return the cord, briefly to each zone in reverse order (brow, heart, navel), and gently wind in your cord, then place it around the back of your neck, holding the ends in each hand.

See sense and feel the Moon Temple all about you, and form a clear intention in your mind that you will return here in your dreams, visions, and meditations.

When you are ready, pass back through the veil and out of the temple.

Now descend the stairs, and return to the outer world.

End of part (2)

Part (3): The Lunar Archangel and the Oceans

Your cord should be around the back of your neck, ends held in right and left hands

Ascend the stairs, as in part (1)

Be still and contemplate the spiritual energies of the lunar realm. Sense, see and feel the radiant Flames, the angels of that realm, as they pass into and out of the manifest world on Earth.

Sense, see and feel the beings that support you on your right and left. They are going to take you into another dimension of this lunar realm. Be still, and let your mind rest upon the intelligence of the archangel Gabriel. Understand this intelligence to be the overmind of the multitude of lunar angels. Gradually the sense of the flowing and streaming angels fades and you come into a vast luminous presence that enfolds you.

Be still, stilling time space and movement. Feel the eternal power of love and compassion that enables all to Be.

Build slowly the image of a vast ocean of water ... see sense and feel its tides, waves, and life-giving presence.

Gradually the water dissolves and the ocean becomes a sea of stars flowing through space and time. Be still, and be at one with that sea, within the enfolding consciousness of the archangel.

(Here you may chant the Call of the West, three times, as you hear it on the CD that accompanies this book)

Now your inner vision changes and you see the sun, moon and earth, as if from beyond our solar system. You are drawn into to the realm of the sun and planets and towards the moon and earth.

Gradually you see your planet Earth and see the extent of ocean that covers her. You are drawn down and down to Earth, towards whichever great ocean is the nearest to your home.

Now you find yourself returning to the place where you began your spiritual journey to the presence of the archangel: you seen sense and feel that place, the building, your own body.

You come back into your outer awareness: sky above, land below, east, south, west, and north.

(Take the cord from your neck, extinguish the candle)

End of part (3)

Let us now consider the presence and power of the Lunar Archangel further, in our context of Cord work.

Understanding the Lunar Archangel

Before reading this, I invite you to clear your mind of what you "know" about angels and archangels. Our contemporary understanding of these intelligences is horribly corrupted and sentimentalised, a process similar to the commercialisation and sentimentalising of the faery realm.

Perhaps the most degraded images nowadays are those of archangels as humanoid entities who enter into trivial relationships with mediums, channellers, and sensitives. If the Archangel Raphael is, apparently, giving you marriage guidance, then it is not Raphael but a poseur, even if it is a spirit poseur with the best of intentions.

To be fair, it might be argued that people of limited perception and intelligence need limited stereotypes in their spiritual lives. I find this line of thought to dangerous, however, and there is little doubt that it often leads to divisive and deluded superiority. Because we live in a time when traditional cultures are fragmenting, when there is no coherent spirituality (either in religion or in sacromagical arts), it is almost impossible to find firm foundations for the inner life. So we must be cautious, as students of the esoteric traditions not to become grandiose.

Having uttered this cautionary preamble, let us move to explore the inner, esoteric, and seldom published nature of the archangel Gabriel. You will find many places where this fits well with popular tradition and others where it becomes more abstract in its metaphysics. We are concerned, always, in this book, with practical applications in Cord work. Before we can work in depth, we have to clear away some barriers of misconception, and lay a foundation of concepts upon which we build. This foundation is, as is always the case in magical arts, derived from the wisdom of our ancestors but not by any means limited to it or dogmatic in its application.

The Cord, the Archangel, and the World

Much of our cord work is in the sub-lunar realm which is the fusion of the consciousness energy and all entities of Moon and Earth. If we can untangle and vivify our spiritual cords here everything else at the solar and stellar levels flows freely and harmoniously. The Archangel Gabriel is traditionally the regent of the Lunar World ... which includes planet Earth. Indeed, this Lunar World intersects with and merges with aspects of the solar world. Traditionally it can include the planets Mercury, Venus, Moon, and Earth, and touches upon the Sun. This is shown in our Figure 8 which is a Tree of Life variant. The Sun also touches the entire Lunar World, of course, with its power: at this stage we are concerned with the lunar spiritual forces, and the intelligence known as Gabriel. They contain a Mystery, for they are not of the Moon alone, but also of the Stars.

During this exploration the archangel is known as "it," not "he": angels and archangels are androgynous...or before polarity...or we might say that they are of a third gender that humans cannot grasp, as it is in a dimension so different from our manifest world of nature. Traditionally Gabriel is the archangel of the Moon, the ocean tides, of conception. Esoterically Gabriel is also the archangel of the tides of death and the life after death. Thus the tides are tides of souls, spirits and consciousness, as well as tides of ocean. Indeed, if we were to restate and reclaim the esoteric definition of this intelligence, it might be best to say that Gabriel in the Archangel of all Tides in the cosmos. The idea that this intelligence is limited to the Lunar realm alone is incorrect and is greatly disempowering in our spiritual lives. It goes along with the modern notion of the lunar consciousness as being somehow inferior, somehow being the dream state or the vague notion of the unconscious mind. None of the foregoing popular ideas come anywhere near close to the true nature of the Archangel Gabriel and the Lunar Realm.

Gabriel is the intelligence, the archangel, that mediates stellar powers into the combined realm of Moon and Earth. Hence for us on earth, Gabriel is most obviously the lunar archangel, and we are most aware of functions that are tidal and of fertility. These are the same functions found in orthodox religious texts: the annunciation in Christianity, the gift of prophecy in Islam, for example. Both show the archangel announcing and enabling the birth of the future. Traditionally we also have Gabriel associated with death and judgement, which derives from the esoteric teaching that it mediates the cosmic forces of another archangel of destruction and purification, into our world of Earth and Moon. We shall return to this theme in the future, in Volume Two, *The Cord of Life and Death.*

The spiritual powers associated with Gabriel are love and compassion from the direction West. This association is of deep significance for us, as the spiritual love and compassion become, so to speak, "humanised" as they flow to us on earth. If we were insects we would find that the spiritual forces becomes "insect-like," for they flow to all living beings equally and each receives and responds according to its own ability to relate, understand and participate.

Thus, in our Cord work, Gabriel is the intelligence that mediates cosmic forces into the cord with something of a *human bias.* This is why, in tradition, the power of love and compassion is associated with spiritual saviours and redeemers and with the compassionate transhuman beings who work with us in the metaphysical realms, and so forth. The archangel mediates the power of love and compassion from the greater world of the cosmos into the smaller world of earth and moon, and by so doing, renders it more human for us. Meditate upon this, and you will have a new understanding of religious motifs such as the Immaculate Conception, and the Annunciation.

Just as the archangel mediates cosmic tides into our sub-lunar world, so does it mediate them out, into the greater world of sun and stars. We hear very little about this in popular spirituality and general religion. For us, as students of sacromagical arts, this tidal flow outwards is especially significant, for we can ride upon it as an aspect of the Evolutionary Stream, as discussed in Chapter 3.

We have now completed the 3 Initiatory Forms. In our next

chapter, a series of short Cord forms is described. These are specific forms that should be undertaken in their own right, but they also apply to many aspects of meditation, visualization, and ritual in which your cord should be present and actively working with you and for you.

Chapter 10:
FURTHER CORD FORMS

1. The Cord of Connection and the Sacred Directions
2. 1st Form: The Stone
3. 2nd Form: The Flame
4. 3rd Form: The Vessel
5. 4th Form: The Altar
6. 5th Form: Earth Light
7. 6th Form: Extending the Directions
8. 7th Form: The Three Zones
9. 8th Form: Earth, Moon, Sun and Stars
10. 9th Form: Fishing in the Well of Light
11. 10th Form: Distance Contact

THE CORD OF CONNECTION AND THE SACRED DIRECTIONS

The following forms are all designed to open out your sense of spiritual connection through and with your cord. They should all be undertaken with your dedicated cord, not limited to solely imaginative or visual exercises. The consciousness must flow through the physical cord.

Before each of form, enter Silence, stilling Time, Space and Movement and then affirm the Seven Directions (East, South, West, North, Above, Below and Center). The center may be within you or the center of a defined Circle, and is, of course, both at One.

1st Form: The Stone

Pass your cord around a stone, holding each end in your right and left hands. Commune with the stone through the cord. As you do this, work to establish a sense of wordless connection with the stone that is deeper than thought or dialogue. Let your essential being and the being of the stone come together harmoniously through the connection of the cord.

The cord will connect you to the stone and the stone to you. There are two modes for working with your cord and a stone:

1. You may think of this as an exercise for the spiritual North: Earth, Stone, Wisdom, Learning and Spirit immanent in matter. Attune to the Temple of the North, the Dark Goddess of transformation, and the powers of the temple of Destruction and Regeneration that flow out of and into all forms.

2. You may think of this as an exercise for the spiritual Center: the stone becomes the Omphalos or navel stone, the Axis Mundi, the pillar of the worlds. It is the marker stone at the Crossroads and reveals Spirit that is fully present in substance at the heart of all things.

2nd Form: The Flame

Pass your cord around a lighted candle. Make sure that the candle is solid and cannot fall over! As in the first form above, hold the ends of the cord and commune. Use the following meditational and ritual form, speaking it aloud whenever possible, or reciting it in your mind while maintaining outer silence. Eventually reduce the words down into their essence, their power. Then, when you speak it aloud, let that power flow out through your voice. You will feel a response flow through the cord and into your body. (This verbal form is included on the CD that accompanies this book.)

This is the terrestrial fire that embodies the Celestial Fire: the candle upon the altar embodies the light of the Stars and Sun. Where it reflects its radiance, it is the Moon.

There are 3 modes for working with your cord and a (pillar) candle:

1. In the South – connecting to the Fire Temple, the cosmic Light of Being, the element of Fire, and the inner contacts of the South, the temple of Initiation and Illumination.

2. In the Center – the candle becomes the Pillar of Light that extends through the Cosmos. Attuning to the heart of the Inner Convocation and the many Priestesses and Priests that work with you in that timeless sacred place.

3. In any of the Four Directions – the candle embodies the power of that Direction and opens the way.

3rd Form: The Vessel

Pass your cord around a bowl or vessel of water and commune as before. There are two modes for this form:

1. In the West – connecting to the Sea Temple, the temple of Giving and Receiving. Attuning to the powers of Love and Compassion that pass in and out with the ebbing and flowing tides.

2. In the Center – the vessel becomes the focus for the cosmic forces of creation, as an embodiment of the vessel of Time, Space and Movement. The water becomes the Ocean of Stars.

In either mode, the water should be used appropriately afterwards. You may drink it or use it for plants. If you have a situation that requires purification, the water can be used for subtle cleansing, after which it must be poured into the earth (not down the drain).

4th Form: The Altar

Let the right and left ends of your cord rest upon the altar, with the center around your neck (you may have to kneel for this) or around your waist. It must be around your body with the open ends on the altar. Commune as before.

There are two modes for this form:

1. In the East – connecting to the Temple of the East, of Instruction and Inspiration. Attuning to the Life forces and the sacred element of Air. Practice breathing steadily and feel the power flow along the cord and into your spine as the air flows in and out of your lungs.

2. In the Center – *Connect to the Ever Becoming that is at the heart of all things, partaking of all shapes, yet bound by none.* Use the simple breathing pattern for the center, as above.

5TH FORM: EARTH LIGHT

Hold one end of the cord and let the other end rest upon the earth. If you are indoors, allow the substance of the building to connect to the Earth, to *be* the Earth. By doing this you can substantially attune and transform a room or building over time. This is a form that begins at the Center, but will conclude with one or more Directions.

You may sit or stand. Feel the cord connect down into the UnderWorld, where it becomes a cord of radiant light reaching into the heart of our planet.

This Earth Light rises up the cord. Initially, let it flow freely through your body, allowing it to build and energize you. But you do not own this power for, when it accumulates, you must freely give it away to all Four Directions to work its mysterious way in the world.

Go to one or more of the Directions to give out the Earth Light that rises up the cord. When you do so, you may have the cord behind you held in one hand, arm downwards, leading back in a line to the Center of the Circle. Your other hand and arm are used to open out the flow of Earth Light, giving it away through your chosen Direction(s).

> NOTE: With practice, this form will build considerable energy and response. Eventually you will be drawn intuitively to one or more Directions for the Giving Forth.

For essential experience and training, you should initially work a cycle of all Four Directions, starting at any one, then completing the cycle in stages. Next, progress to working all Four in one session.

6TH FORM: EXTENDING THE DIRECTIONS

Extend the end of the Cord into one of the Directions, commune and exchange. You can do this standing or sitting. Work a cycle of the Four Directions, one during each session. Build up to doing all Four in one Session. Then return to one at a time (four sessions) then all four in one session.

7TH FORM: THE THREE ZONES

This form relates to the forms 5 and 6. However, start this Form when you have practiced the others and feel familiar with them.

One end of the Cord is placed before you on the ground or floor. This is the Center. You may sit or stand. Link with the rising Earth Light, as in Form 5 above. There are three stages to this Form:

1. Hold the Cord with both hands against your navel (loins and genitals). Feel the Earth Light flow into your body. You may feel it circulating and flowing in both directions along the cord. Be still and commune.

2. Hold the cord with both hands against your heart zone (heart and lungs). Commune and allow circulation of Earth Light.

3. Hold the cord with both hands against your brow (forehead, above the nose). Commune and allow circulation.

Then, reverse the pattern: head, heart and loins, back to Earth.

8th Form: Earth, Moon, Sun and Stars

(A shorter version of this form, without the cord element, was first published in *The Miracle Tree, Demystifying Qabalah*.)

This form may be undertaken while sitting, standing or walking. Your cord should be around your waist, tied with a loose double knot with ends towards the front. If you are using this form as a walking meditation and do not wish to attract attention to yourself, concealed the cord and omit the movements described for the ends of the cord in each part of the working.

Begin by being still, stilling Time, Space and Movement.

1. Sit or stand facing East. Affirm each Direction about you: East, South, West, North, Sky Above, Land Below and Being Within.

2. Direct your awareness to your feet: "My feet are of the Earth." Feel the *physical* Earth power flow through your feet. Lower the ends of your cord to the Earth, touching the ground for a moment and then your feet. Rise slowly towards the next part ...

3. Direct your awareness to your genitals: "My genitals are of the Moon." Feel the power rise into your genitals and, at the same time and visualize the Lunar power descending from the *physical* Moon to merge with it. Touch your cord to your genitals. Rise slowly towards the next part.

4. Direct your awareness to your center, your heart: "My heart is of the Sun." Feel the combined Earth and Lunar power rise into your Heart and visualize the Solar power descending from the *physical* Sun to merge with it. While standing upright, touch your cord to your heart.

5. Direct your awareness to your head: "My head is in the Stars." Feel the combined Earth, Lunar and Solar forces rise into the Head. Visualize the Stellar power descending from the *physical* stars to merge with it. Touch your cord to your brow.

6. Be still, silent and poised. Feel the perfect balance of these

physical and spiritual forces within you, between Above and Below at the Center of the Directions.

7. Walking mode – Begin to walk in any direction. As you walk, connect to Earth, Moon, Sun and Stars, through the zones of your body as described above. Omit the cord movements and allow the ends of your cord to fall free as you walk.

Closing: Briefly repeat the pattern, touching the ends of the cord to each zone of the body. Affirm the Directions again and make the Crossing Sign (touch the top of your forehead for Above/Cosmos, touch your navel for Below/Earth, your right shoulder for Breadth/Justice, your left shoulder for Fullness/Mercy. Circle and enclose all four points by circling your hand sunwise. Draw in the directions and be still.) Your meditation is complete.

9th Form: Fishing in the Well of Light

In this form we use our cords in conjunction with the Well of Light that opens from the source of Earth Light, deep in the planetary body and energy. A full set of workings with the Well of Light can be found in *The Well of Light*.

Once you have opened the Well of Light, let your cord pass downwards into the Earth Light. Feel the subtle energies flowing from the cord into your body. You may also use the cord to make contact with Go-Betweens or ancestral contacts. Just as the cord makes the contact, it also enhances and modulates it, keeping the subtle forces in balance. When you wish to conclude the contact, draw the cord back and close the Well of Light.

10th Form: The Distance Contact Form

A simple cord form for making distance contact.

Many people expect that distance contact will work somewhat like television, as if we see a picture of whatever we are seeking on some kind of screen. Older accounts of distance contact (written before television) are, therefore, often misinterpreted through the ubiquitous influence of television upon modern life. The popular notion of the crystal ball and of "scrying" is similar to watching something on television in most contemporary descriptions. Yet this is not what was undertaken, experienced or described by the magicians of earlier generations.

For example, traditional use of the crystal emphasizes that the crystal causes a painful light to expand within the head of the user, and that this light contains visions. It is often sought at first as a twinkling star inside the crystal which then opens out as the light within the awareness of the user. This is very different to the idea that pictures appear like television news footage inside the crystal ball.

When you work with this cord form for distance contact, be aware that the contact experiences will work in many different ways: touch, smell, sight and hearing may all be involved. Most often what we find is a totality of shared comprehension: you know and share, momentarily, a wide range of sensations, intimations and perceptions. These can be of a person, of a place, of a situation. The problem is not one of making or opening out contact, as we can all do that easily. It is one of limiting and focusing the contact.

If we pause to think for a moment, we discover that this limiting of contact is something that we have been doing all our lives, and which we do all the time. This limiting and focusing is, in truth, what creates the individual sense of time and place. If we were open to anything and everything, as seems to be the case in some types of schizophrenia or autism, then we would not be able to function in the consensual world of modern humanity.

The following cord form will help you to make distance contact and to limit and balance it in ways that are appropriate for you. Remember, each individual works, sends and receives in different ways. This cord form allows for that individuality.

1. Light a candle flame and still your sense of time, space and movement. Be at peace.

2. Hold one end of your cord in both hands. Cast the other end out as if you are fishing (which is exactly what you are doing).

3. When the cord falls to Earth, sense that the other end is touching whatever you wish to perceive. NOTE: do not attempt to build this up before you cast your cord.

4. Work the contact through your three main zones of consciousness: the loins, the heart and the head. This is done by placing the end of the cord that you hold upon each zone in turn. You will connect with your subject in different ways according to each zone. Do not strain, do not concentrate. Simply be aware that the other end of your cord is touching whatever you seek to perceive.
You may make brief notes after each zone, but do not break the cord contact while you are doing so. Keep them as brief as possible so that they are clues for a more thorough set of notes after you have completed the cord form. In each case, keep the cord on the zone with one hand, while writing the notes with another. You could easily use a small voice-activated recorder during this phase, and thus keep both hands on the cord.

5. Now bring in the far end of your cord, detaching it from the subject.

6. Place the cord around the back of your neck, holding the ends in your right and left hand. Lift your cord up to the Moon, Sun and Stars (Above). Extend your cord to the Earth (Below). Place the ends and both hands upon your heart (Within). As you make this threefold movement, come into balance.

7. Conclude by being still, stilling time, space and movement. Put out the candle and take off your cord, putting it away in a bag or on your altar.

You can now expand your notes from memory if you wish.

CAUTION: do not over-use this method. Do not try it for long periods of time and do not try to force it. It has a natural rhythm and pace that you will discover with practice.

Once you are versed in these short forms, you will find many further ways of applying them in your spiritual life and work. As always with such techniques, they should be regarded as open-ended, for they are capable of infinite development and inner transformation if we stay with them diligently. We are ready now to proceed to the last chapter concerning the Cord of Death.

CHAPTER 11:
THE CORD OF DEATH

1. Birth Cord, Death Cord
2. Participation in Death
3. Making a Death Cord
4. Death and Personality
5. Physical Life after Death
6. Coherence of Personality After Death
7. Strong Personalities: Positive and Negative

In this last chapter we will explore some cord work and concepts concerning death and the process of dying. This theme will be the focus for our second book, *The Cord of Life and Death*, which will offer in-depth cord forms and teachings for the transitions of death that we must all undergo.

By now you will be familiar with our series of basic cord forms and empowered visions. Remember that a Place is a state of consciousness and you will come to know everything necessary for awareness of and during death. Working with a cord substantially assists us in our experience of death and of the dying process, be it that of another person or our own. This assistance can also be applied to the death of any being, any situation, and is not limited to purely human concerns. In our present context, however, we will discuss the human concerns over death and how a cord may assist with this process of transformation.

Birth Cord, Death Cord

We are born with a cord, we die with a cord. In humans the birth cord has a special manifestation, connecting organically between the infant and mother, just as all beings are connected, metaphysically to the Great Mother of universal being. The death cord does not seem, to us, to have an organic presence but we can use a physical cord and its astral double to create such a presence. In both cases the organic birth cord of cells and blood, and the substitute death cord of organic fibres and astral light, there is a connection to the spine. It is our spinal cord that carries the outer manifestation of our spirit cord ... into this world, through this world and out of this world.

Of course the spinal cord decays at death and ceases to serve the physical functions for which it was designed. But the astral cord does not cease or decay. This is why we place much emphasis upon the development and nourishment of the astral cord through intentional spiritual work. As mentioned in chapter 4, which discusses the astral double of the cord, all beings that manifest in form or in nature can and do generate astral doubles. Usually these doubles rise and fall like the grass or cycle through ages like the stars and in all cases the process is, initially, unconscious and the entity/being, human or other, does not relate consciously with its astral double. Partly as a result of this unconsciousness, the double is greatly involved in the process of rebirth, be it of a single cell or of a stellar nebula. The astral double holds an image or imprint which confers a certain degree of continuity at rebirth. In an "unconscious" being, the continuity can become repetitive patterns which imprint from the astral double into the sub-lunar world and thus into the outer life. Or, to put it more simply, until we become more fully conscious our lives seem to go around in circles. This should remind us of the ancient philosophical exercise of the cord and the peg that was described at the beginning of this book.

Participation in Death

We can work with this continuity/imprint function of the astral double intentionally, in our Cord practices. The difference is one of intention and awareness … the double builds, functions and regenerates even if we are not aware of it. But if we work with it consciously we begin to participate in the cosmos, rather than remain unwitting of the greater life and consciousness. There are many implications to this action of the astral double and the possibility of working with it consciously. These implications are of special significance to us when we participate in death, perhaps working with another person or being who is dying, or for ourselves.

This participation in death is the subject of our last chapter and the theme for the second volume. We can explore some practical work here, at the close of this first volume, ranging from methods of assisting someone who is dying, to methods that will be beneficial for our own transition out of this world into another. Three main topics arise:

1. Making a death cord for another person
2. Working with your long term cord at the close of your life
3. Entering the inner temples at death

All of these, and a number of others not listed here, will be discussed, explored and demonstrated in depth in the next book. At this stage, let us consider some practical work with each of the three listed above.

Making a Death Cord

This is something that is done for another and not for yourself. It must be done with permission and with some involvement of the person who is dying. There can be one exception, when that person is in a coma and cannot be conscious. We will return to this exception shortly.

Here is an example of how a death cord will be helpful.

Talk with the person who is approaching death. Ask him/her to consider making a cord to help with a peaceful death. Even if the person is in pain, this is the aim of making the cord.

At this stage, the cord can be made physically in several different ways. The individual may want very strongly to make his/her own cord, or at least to have a length of braided or woven cord to work with. This is probably the best method, but of course, it is not always possible.

1. Discuss the cord concept in simple direct ways that are non-religious and non-specialised. Encourage your friend or relative to contemplate their life, and to tie some knots in the cord for key events, relationships, joys and griefs. Some people will want to tie many knots while others will only have a few. Discuss how, if there are many knots, they could be reduced down to a few wherever possible.

2. Encourage your friend or relative to hold the cord and pass their hands over the knots. If possible he/she should meditate with, or at least think upon, why they tied each knot. This is the first stage. There is no set timing to these stages and you can help with them, but help minimally and do not try to interfere or impose.

3. The next stage is for the person to work again with the knots and to consider and imagine untying them. They are untied with love, with forgiveness. The physical knots themselves are not untied at this time but the individual begins to understand that as he/she dies these knots can be consciously untied with love and forgiveness.

At this stage, depending upon circumstances, some knots will be more difficult to untie than others. You may help with this, if such help is agreed upon. You can help through simple talk, or through shared meditations on relationships, love and compassion. Especially focus on letting go, on untying, in peace. De-emphasize sentiment and clinging through fear; the individual is dying and to sentimentalize the process is to insult and trivialise him or her.

The touching of the physical knots is often satisfying and fulfilling in ways that exceed talking or even meditating. Ideally touching the knots and silent meditation upon their content is best. Some people, however, will want to talk, maybe even confess regarding each knot or regarding certain knots. Let them do so, be a good listener and pass no judgements. The person who is dying will soon meet the ultimate judge of his/her life ... their true self after death, beyond personality.

4. Undoing the knots. If possible the individual should gradually begin to undo the knots. This should not be rushed, and can be done over a number of days if possible (we will explore what can be done if he/she cannot undo the knots themselves next).

Traditionally this is done in reverse order to the tying. If the knots were tied from the early life to the present, they are untied in reverse order. Thus the knots are untied back towards birth. Sometimes many memories arise when this is done especially of early life. Such memories are often radiant with the light and innocence of childhood ... this is part of the death process.

With each knot the person asks for and gives forgiveness, if necessary, and unties with the aim of releasing joys and pains equally. This is not an easy task but the physical untying greatly assists therein.

5. When the last knot is undone (usually something from childhood or early life), encourage your friend or relative to work with a Stillness meditation.

6. Do not expect someone to die when the last knot is gone, nor should he/she expect it to be so. This might be the ideal and may indeed happen, but it is important not to feel a sense of anticlimax after the last knot is untied. Usually it brings peace, readiness and calm. The physical death will come but the knots have been untied now and the individual is as ready as he or she may be.

7. What if he/she cannot untie the knots, if, for example they die before this task is complete, or if they are unable to untie them for health reasons? In this case, if you have worked with the person and know something of what is in the knots, you may untie them. Do not do this if the person has even the faintest ability to do it for themselves, no matter how slow or uncertain they may be. If you

do this untying, feel the person with you and you untie the knots together. When the last knot is untied, you bid them farewell.

In some situations, you may know very little about the knots. In such a case, assert in meditation that you are untying, unconditionally, for the person who tied them. When you do this, feel that person with you, and especially sense that they can feel the knots through your hands. When you have undone the last knot, even though you have no knowledge of it, their presence will fade.

8. What do we do with the cord that was made, tied, and untied? As a rule you should burn or bury this cord with the person who has died. It must not be kept by a friend or family member, as this creates unhealthy sentiment that may inhibit the beloved dead from passing into new realms of consciousness. Sentiment, grief, and selfishness all act as anchors that prohibit release. If we truly love someone, we let them go. If we cling to them, we are only really loving ourselves.

9. There is a related cord form that family members and loved ones can do which is to make a cord for themselves to assist in letting go of the person who has died. This is done only after the death, not before. You simply tie a few knots in a cord, one for each key idea, event or connection between you and the other who has recently died. In simple calm meditation, identify each knot and untie it. You can release much in yourself, and much that ties another after death, by doing this. When the knots have all gone, burn the cord and bury the ashes.

Death and Personality

What happens to the habitual personality on the death of the physical body?

The accepted view is that once the body has died, the personality no longer functions. Indeed, it is demonstrable that it cannot function in the habitual manner, for the body no longer functions, hence there is no outlet, vehicle or means, whereby the personality may express itself. The body is, typically, regarded as waste to be disposed. Of course, there are many cultural ceremonies around this disposal of the body ranging from complex respect and grieving rituals to a simple utilitarian approach.

It is customary at this point to enter into cultural or religious assumptions, teachings, and traditions, regarding the consciousness and personality of the deceased. In the modernist, post-Christian era, this personality is regarded atheistically, as having ceased. In a religious context there are varied teachings about an entity of soul or spirit that "leaves the body." Yet these typical descriptions, be they materialist or spiritual, omit several important ideas regarding what happens after death. These may be demonstrated through the processes that occur within the body itself, from an organic viewpoint, rather than from a perspective or belief or metaphysics. Let us explore some of them now:

Firstly, we need to be aware that the body is not entirely "dead," and that there are many stages of death of the organism that progress after the initial moment that we typify as death when the vital organs cease to function. Such stages of death effect a steady winding down of the body as a co-operative entity and comprise its separation into many smaller entities or life-forms that no longer co-operate as the whole human body. In a symbolic sense we might think of this as a matter of *direction*. After death, the body disperses, moving outwards and away from its center or integral identity. Before death it rhythmically coheres, always cycling inwards to its centre, to maintain a certain integrity and identity. In both cases, the movement affects entity. At death we have a movement away from the Body and Organs, a movement of Micro-organisms. At conception and during development we have a movement towards the body, of Micro-organisms, that build Organs and thus the body itself. This is due to the action of the Involuntary and Evolutions streams which is described in our Chapter 3.

This separation and dispersion at death, this complex and immense life-after-death that we seldom consider will be influenced, of course, by what is done with the body. Is it buried, cremated or frozen? In some cases the body is frozen before burial or cremation and this changes the natural rhythm of the separation referred to above. We might think of this separation and dispersion as a return to primal life forms, just as the fertilized cells and the embryo are often described as recapitulating a passage from primal life forms into the complex interactions of organs and whole body, in an ongoing process of cohesion. *This cohesion and dispersion of the body as a co-operative collective is mirrored in the increasing coherence of the individual personality that develops during life, and in its dispersion, and progressive incoherence, after death.*

Before going further we should note that the "death" forces and the "life" forces are simultaneous in every stage of human development from conception to bodily death. Once a body has started on its path towards form and expression, it dies and is renewed at a cellular level in a ceaseless dance of destruction and creation. Indeed, contemplating this dance transforms our habitual conditioned or popular notions of death substantially.

Physical Life after Death

After the cessation of vital signs and functions the body returns to basics, giving itself over to the cleansing and reducing forces of earth. These are, of course, typically identified as forces of "decay" or "corruption" to use the old English word. In truth they are forces of re-cycling. If a body is buried, its dispersing elements (micro-organisms) pass out into the earth and eventually re-combine with other elements to form and nourish other entities. In a small community (such as we do not have in modernist culture) the other members of the community may eventually be nourished by sources of sustenance that include elements from the dispersed dead bodies of those that have gone before, even to the extent of foodstuffs. In the modernist world, we may still find traces of such nourishment in the air, the water and (less often) in other life forms.

All of the foregoing is of deep significance when we consider what happens to the personality after death, for the dispersal of the body is mirrored by a dispersal of the personality.

COHERENCE OF PERSONALITY AFTER DEATH

As a simple rule it seems that the stronger the personality, the more likely it is to endure after physical death. Let us examine this idea in detail for there are many implications therein. What is typically thought of as "strength of personality" rests upon a sense of identity and there are many ways in which this sense of self can be patterned during a lifetime. Indeed, depending upon the strength, the sense of self and how it is identified to itself, within itself, the death process will vary considerably. This is not surprising for the same changes and variations occur in the development and decline of the personality in life.

For example, someone who is an athlete with a strong self-image founded upon physical prowess and victory in competition has to undergo many changes when he or she matures and can no longer compete. The urge to excellence may be transmuted into other activities such as coaching, or in other fields of endeavor altogether. A man who loses his executive job may feel, or even become, impotent. A man or woman going through divorce can loose that sense of self that was built in the marriage, the family or the world of that particular life-phase. In all such examples, the personality can adapt and reform upon the foundation of its experiences, or the individual may lose their sense of self-worth and/or their image of themselves and decline. This type of pattern is well known to therapists, who work with those who have lost their "sense of self" arising from changes in their life.

In all such cases there is a strong "outward" focus, into the arena of human life and the role whereby the individual identifies his or her self. Many people have little inner strength but draw a strong sense of self from a role … athlete, executive, mother, career and so forth. It may be that, over time, an inner strength gradually develops from experience, especially if the personality is open to change.

Such outwardly focused personalities may cling to the dramatic, or symbolic, token-based self-image after death. In rare cases this may be attached to intense emotion leading to the phenomenon of resonance, imprinting, or "haunting" which is always linked to a specific location wherein the personality had some significant experiences. We will return to this theme of imprints later.

The outwardly focused personality may be able to resist the natural forces of dispersal that occur at death. Through concentrating upon the self-image, this personality is able to endure and remain at least partly coherent, counter to the tide of dispersal that is flowing through the body. However, the basic natural process is one in which the tide of physical dispersal after "death" is mirrored in a dispersal of the personality. Just as the senses fade, organ by organ (usually with hearing as the last) in the dying process, so do concomitant aspects of the personality fade and disperse after death. The "strong" personality which may, in truth, be weak in its depths and only strong in its determination to hold to a symbolic sense of identity, often fights the tide. But as the organs of the body decline before death, bringing a reduction of the classic senses, so does the tide of dispersal after death bring a reduction of the sense of self. After all, there is no longer a body to work with and the functions of memory, so important in the sense of self of an outward focused person in old age, are therefore inhibited and progressively inaccessible. Hence the symbolic sense of self ... as something emblematic or as a collection of desires which were significant during life, even though it has no outer means of expression.

As the vital forces of the body decline, and the tide flows Outwards, away from coherence, the symbolic personality no longer has sources of sustenance. It can fade and flow away with the tide, or it can fight to remain as an entity. This struggle is well known in tradition and many of the death and disposal rituals are intended to deal with it in a harmonious, loving and compassionate manner. The idea of the wake as a farewell party is a good example. The deceased personality is honored and is brought to understand that he or she really is dead, and is *fed and sustained* during the happy party. Then the ritual of burial opens the way for the tides of dispersal and everyone lets go, both the living and dead.

If we are to find a new approach to death for the 21st century, we have to consider the following:

1. Preparation for death
2. Working through the death process itself
3. Preparation for after-death consciousness
4. Working through the after-death processes
5. Disposing of fear and ignorance in stages 1-4

STRONG PERSONALITIES, POSITIVE AND NEGATIVE

A different strength of personality is found in those who did not live their lives dependent upon roles and outer patterns but found inner strength that sustained them even during their darkest most shattered phases of life. These may include people with spiritual interests and practices, creative and innovative artists and scientists, and those who have lived simply and in harmony with the ceaseless tides of life and death. There is often less fear of death among such persons but there is still a strong personality that survives. They may be identified in two main categories: those who rest upon their inner strength to remain coherent after death (in despite of the tides of dispersal) and those who use that inner strength as a foundation, a starting place for letting go of the old persona and exploring new conditions.

In our second volume, *The Cord of Life and Death* we will explore the death process further, especially in the context of Cord work and individual continuity between lives. Further aspects of this continuity include participation within the Inner Temples, conscious co-operation upon the Evolutionary Stream and continuity of purpose through many lives.

CONCLUSION

1. Work Towards Goals, but Do Not Identify with Them
2. The Cord Works for You in Three Ways
3. The Spindle or Spinning Top
4. The Cord Enhances All Our Spiritual Practices

Cord work is open-ended and ongoing; there is no "end" or "goal." Indeed, most true spiritual work is not goal-orientated, despite popular literature to the contrary. If we achieve a goal, our purpose has ended from that point on and, like hungry ghosts, we are immediately seeking the next target of purpose and gratification. Only when we have no self-acclaimed purpose can we begin to be aware of our true nature. Understanding this concept is especially difficult for us, as it is often confused with passivity or negativity. An interim way of understanding is to consider that the goal or purpose is no longer an outward seeking achievement but an inner transformation.

WORK TOWARDS GOALS, BUT DO NOT IDENTIFY WITH THEM

This curious problem of being obsessively goal-driven is endemic in modernist culture where false goals and artificial values are the chains, shackles and whips of psychic and emotional slavery. A classic example is that of the career man or woman who loses a job or retires and then falls apart. Self cannot be identified with goals, no matter how temporarily reassuring goal achievement may be. *The secret is to work towards goals, but not to identify with them.* In spiritual practice the goals are often in service and compassion, with little or no self-benefit. At the deeper levels of spiritual practice, the goals are long-term involving the collective consciousness and its movement on the evolutionary stream that radiates off-planet. We will return to this theme in Volume Two, *The Cord of Life and Death.*

When we die, and at any moment of conscious living, the sum of a life is not the achievements but rather the consciousness that results from the effort made while working on those achievements. We take that sum of consciousness with us when we die, but we do not take the ephemeral achievements themselves. We are all aware, of course, of the popular truth that being immensely rich means little if you are miserable, aggressive, bitter and vindictive. This is the classic "achievement truth," but there are many variations, some being extremely subtle.

THE CORD WORKS FOR YOU IN THREE WAYS

In regular practice the Cord will work for you in three ways. You have now completed the initiatory phases that empower and connect your physical Cord, and now have reconnected to the astral double of your Cord.

1. *Strengthening and clarifying altered consciousness* using the methods and your interaction with the inner contacts that you have encountered as a result of Cord work. These are all described in our preceding chapters which provide a resource for ongoing work with the Cord. The basic forms cannot be outgrown, for they are open-ended. The more we work with them, the more effective they become and we discover new ways to apply them in practice.

2. *Opening the way to new experiences and inner contacts* that are not fully described in our text. The open-ended forms will lead you into new awareness as you continue to work with them. Eventually you will be able to condense each form into a focused mode of awareness which acts as a vehicle for reaching deep into the greater awareness, both of our world and of others.

3. *The physical cord acts as a stabilizer.* This is one of the most helpful aspects of using a physical cord in regular practice and daily life. As you wear it, the empowered and contacted cord will make minute ongoing adjustments to your consciousness and energy. Over time, these subtle adjustments will also be detected in your physical body, especially in the pelvis, spine, neck and skull.

THE SPINDLE OR SPINNING TOP

An analogy of balance-in-motion was used in spiritual teaching from the most ancient times illustrated with the classic demonstration of a spinning top. The cosmic allegory, found in Plato's *Republic*, can be demonstrated by the use of a stick, cord and spinning top. The stick is the distaff of the Goddess. The cord attached to the distaff winds around the spindle of the spinning top. When the cord is pulled to create spin, the distaff applies energy to the motion of the top, keeping it balanced, upright and rotating.

This model holds true for the cosmos, the solar system, our planet Earth, and the human being. Without the rotating energy, the balanced system falls apart.

THE CORD ENHANCES ALL OUR SPIRITUAL PRACTICES

Wearing the cord in meditation and sleeping with it helps us to remember and connect through the body and to stay balanced. It helps us to not slide backwards through daily stresses and forgetfulness. Most of all, the cord enhances all our spiritual practices once we have opened to its potential and empowered our physical cords.

In this book we have explored some of the inner esoteric teachings that are hardly ever published or taught, and have established a training pattern for cord work that will last you for many years. The rest is up to you.

R.J. Stewart
Vashon Island, WA
October 2005

APPENDIX 1: THE RIVERS OF BLOOD AND TEARS

(First published in *The Cauldron*, Nov 2004, UK. See *The Cauldron* website at http://www.the-cauldron.fsnet.co.uk/)

The UnderWorld Initiation, the Crossroads, and the Rivers of Tears and Blood Revisited

Prefatory note to the reader: This essay deals with only one branch of the UnderWorld Initiation, that of the Scottish faery tradition. There are other branches, ranging from those of the classical ancient Mediterranean world, to Northern European, to the shamanistic traditions. They all have certain themes, motifs and magical concepts in common.

I have not peppered this article with extensive academic style footnotes and references. If you intend detailed research, you can find footnotes and references aplenty in the books or websites that I cite below

THE UNDERWORLD INITIATION

Back in the late 1970s I wrote a book entitled *The UnderWorld Initiation*[1]. It was not intended for publication and was circulated privately to a small network of friends and fellow workers of magic. Gareth Knight, however, suggested to Aquarian Press (always honest Aquarian, like all publishers) that they might print it, and by the mid to late 1980s the book had gone through several editions and changes of cover, and has remained in print in various incarnations to this day. It led to subsequent books: *Earth Light, Power Within the Land*[2] and *The Well of Light*, written and published between 1985 and 2004. All of these books describe methods, experiences and metaphysical patterns founded on the simple ideas of a) exploring and respecting ancestral tradition and b) enacting its content in practical magic.

The idea of intentionally and consciously entering the UnderWorld through visionary or ritual methods, and then communing with the occupants therein, was by no means widespread in paganism and magic up to the early 1980s. Indeed, it was shunned and repudiated, and we will return to some aspects of this repudiation later in this article. Very few, if any, of the older generation who were my teachers used such methods. I say this with respect, for without their mentorship, I would not have been able to explore as I have. Each generation finds the magic that is needful for its time, place and transformation.

Nowadays, to my mixed pleasure and chagrin, I find material from my UnderWorld books appearing in many places and claimed as "traditional" material; I receive letters or emails from strange persons claiming to have learned it all from their grandmothers or that they have been teaching it for 30 years, but only just read it in *Earth Light* last week. In an age of rank commercialism, such people often have an angle, but others are truly inspired and resonate with the older traditions. Perhaps the most bizarre example is that one of my original UnderWorld visualization texts, provably published some years ago, is quoted without acknowledgement in an expensive course on aromatherapy! Things have certainly changed since I labored over that old typewriter and produced that clunky book.

Prior to *The UnderWorld Initiation*, there seemed to be very few themes on folkloric UnderWorld magic in general use within the magical or spiritual revival. Today they are substantially more widespread. Not, I hasten to add, because of this one book, or because of subsequent expositions in some of my later books, but because that first book was part of a greater shift of consciousness.

I claim ownership of my own texts and teaching methods, but only the ancestors own the traditions.

This shift of consciousness to which I refer is, in part, our liberation from the suppression and conditioning of the Christian and post-Christian modernist programs. But more significantly, it is also the sign of a greater change. The older traditions of magic are gradually coming back in new and potent forms.

WHAT ARE WE, AS HUMANS?

There is a core idea in all faery/UnderWorld/Earth-based spirituality, which I would like to state. It is so obvious, so factual, so directly undeniable and self evident. Yet, it is so easily forgotten. It is this: *We have no life without our planet Earth.*

This essential earthliness is the *Foundation* described in traditional Qabalah, in Renaissance theosophy and magic, and in the bardic magical cosmology of the medieval Merlin texts. Nowadays we find that the Foundation is loosely described as the Moon, lunar or subconscious realm in popular books on Qabalah and magic, but this is inaccurate. Strictly the Foundation is the Earth and Moon joined, cohabiting and resonating together. The Moon orbits and weaves a sphere around Earth, and thus they are really a coherent entity. The Earth is inside the Moon, if you but pause to think about it. Everything that we experience, everything that we are, our entire consciousness and energy is within the vast consciousness and energy field of the combined, interacting Earth and Moon. This statement is neither "occultism" nor speculation, it is a material fact. The combined forces, the sphere of Earth and Moon, include and enfold all planetary consciousness, which is that of countless trillions of living creatures from microbes to whales. Every thought, every impulse that you have is within the field of many other living beings ... both physical and, according to the ancestral traditions, metaphysical.

So how did we end up with dogmatic religions and spirituality that reject and deny the very essence of our being? No need to answer.

The key to UnderWorld spirituality is to consciously acknowledge where we are and what we are. When we do this, we discover how to break down the conditioned barriers of human limited awareness, blinkered, straight-jacketed, and cruelly mute. The methods for this cleansing are preserved in folkloric traditional magic ... our task is not merely to research this and restate it, but to experience it, to *do* it, as contemporary people. In this sense we are not individuals seeking the monstrous ego-beast of "self development," but we stand for humanity, acting for those who cannot yet act for themselves, seeing for those that cannot yet see, speaking to spiritual worlds for those that do not yet have a voice.

By "folkloric traditional magic" I mean those anonymous methods and practices and images that have been handed down in oral tradition through the centuries. At certain times these have been preserved in threshold texts that offer us evidence of continuity of the old traditions[3]. Much of this material involves going down into, and passing through, the body of the land, thereby entering a metaphysical realm and encountering its inhabitants. We find such motifs very widespread, from ancient classical temple traditions to modern folktales. This is, in short, the transformative process that I entitled, back in 1978, *The UnderWorld Initiation*.

The entire sacro-magical process of the UnderWorld can be summarized very simply: *go there and participate*. Both the methodology and the road map for this are clearly defined in tradition, and the rest of this article is a short and reasonably simple outline of those definitions. They involve, but are by no means limited to the following: the Crossroads, the Two Rivers, the UnderWorld Tree, and the Return.

BEGINNING AND ENDING AT THE CROSSROADS

First and last, in all spiritual magic, we have the idea of the Crossroads. Traditionally this must be a physical crossroads;

modern magicians, pagans and occultists place far too much emphasis on magic "in the mind," a problem that has been created by the materialist science of psychology. In old-fashioned magic you could not go to the Crossroads of spirit until you had been to the physical crossroads and worked with the allies, cousins and co-walkers that met you there. This is the core of the old faery tradition ... a rather frightening and cathartic tradition that bears no relationship to the contemporary cutsie-pie nonsense that we see so widely touted in recent books, New Age art, and on the Internet. The faery allies, cousins and co-walkers are frightening, cathartic, loving and ecstatic ... but frightening and cathartic *first*.

The Crossroads[4] is used in traditional magic for meeting the faery races, the ancestors and the spiritual forces of our living planet. The outer Crossroads, usually experienced at midnight, is always mirrored by an inner crossroads. But you cannot substitute the outer experience with an inner fantasy: the crossroads must be a real experience. The inner crossroads arise, of course, whenever we have life-crises. In old fashioned magic, you "got it all out" at the physical crossroads, intentionally and willingly, albeit fearfully. If we really do this, wholeheartedly, we gradually lose our fear and have less difficulty with our inner crossroads. This is not, I hasten to add, materialist psychology, but the practical and highly effective magical and spiritual psychology of the older traditions. When it comes to understanding of consciousness, 19th and 20th century materialist psychology has tried to re-invent the wheel ... resulting in a model that is horribly incomplete and inadequate by comparison to the psychology of the perennial spiritual traditions.

But when you are at the Crossroads, you do not "get it all out" alone ... the cathartic transactions involve the presence of, and communion with, spirit beings. These take many forms: the *genii loci*, the traditional allies, cousins and co-walkers of the faery realm, the ancestors, the older gods and goddesses, the titan or giant beings that embody the consciousness and energy of huge geomantic or telluric zones, and so forth. After the catharsis, we are able to discover the Other Crossroads. Not as some imaginary exercise or associative meandering under the cunning skill of a well-paid therapist, but as a potent reality into which we enter fully, openly and with no thought of holding back.

THE CROSSROADS IN THE UNDERWORLD

The faery tradition stipulates and offers that we have to go to the physical crossroads to meet our terrifying and loving allies who bring us into a clearer sense of the land, the ocean and the planet, thereby removing our human shackles, and opening us to our true power and place on Earth.

The UnderWorld Crossroads is then open to us and this is the realm of Prophecy. The basic map for this is clearly described in the Scottish traditional ballad of *Thomas Rhymer*. Indeed, you only need two ballads to encompass and practice the entire faery and UnderWorld tradition: *Thomas Rhymer* and *Tam Lin*. So throw away those dreary R.J. Stewart books now!

In the UnderWorld, the Crossroads is where potentials come together, and a locus from which potentials emerge. Thomas is shown a Tree growing at the Crossroads by his initiatrix, the Queen of Elfland. We will return to this Tree shortly. It is this source of *potentials,* experienced at the Crossroads, which brings, for us as humans, prophecy. Thomas Rhymer serves in the UnderWorld for seven years, after which he is given gifts ... one of these is the tongue that cannot lie. The historical Thomas of Erceldoune or Earlston, by the way, made many accurate local predictions, most of which came about after his death in the 13th century. His influence is found, curiously, in Shakespeare's *Macbeth*, written in 1606 some 250 or more years after the death of Thomas Earlston[5].

Whereas the manifest crossroads is an embodiment on the Earth of the Four Directions of East, South, West and North, the UnderWorld crossroads is an embodiment of *directions of consciousness*. Furthermore, it is an embodiment of the collectives, streams, hyper-organisms of specific orders of life on Earth. These are: Human (including ancestors), Faery, and Living Creature (including all non-human organic life forms).

"Wait," I hear you shout … "that is only Three Roads!" Indeed so … the Crossroads in the UnderWorld has only three branches. On the surface, the crossroads arise because of the poles of North and South, and the rotation of the planet that generates our subjective ideas of East and West (sunrise and sunset). This gives us four directions: two are objective (North and South) and two are subjective (East and West). Plus, of course, the essential Above and Below created in our consciousness by the power of gravity. In truth there is no Above, only *around* or *enfolding the planet*, and likewise there is no Below, but only *within the planet*.

If you are serious about your magical work, you can bring profound changes of awareness by working with these ideas of Around and Within, rather than Above and Below. When I use Above and Below in my own work, I conceive of them, always, as being around the planet and within the planet. This helps to dispose of our conditioned naïve dualism, inherited willy-nilly from Christian suppression.

In the UnderWorld, as we know from tradition, sunrise and sunset do not occur. This is true, of course, in a physical sense beneath the earth. But we are taught that there is, traditionally, star light and earth light; that same light described by the Scottish witch Isobel Gowdie who, dear soul, told her prosecutors that she had traveled to a radiant place in the center of the Earth, where she dined with the faery king and queen. This light, either of mysterious stars or issuing directly out of the Earth, is also described in many faery tales and legends concerning the UnderWorld and Faery Realm.

Thus the four roads, defining a relationship of space, time and movement (planetary poles, rotation, and the resulting day, night and seasons), become three roads of consciousness in the UnderWorld. Let us now briefly examine these Roads:

In the ballad of *Thomas Rhymer*, our traditional example of faery initiation and exposition, they are called the Path of Wickedness, the Path of Righteousness and the Path to Elfland. The Roads are further defined as the Broad Way, the Narrow Way and the Bonny Middle Way.

In an esoteric sense they represent 1) Humanity, 2) Living

Creatures and 3) Faery races as paths or modes or collectives of consciousness.

1. Wickedness or worldliness is typical to humanity – today we would surely call it modernism. No other order of life on Earth has this. This is the broad and easy way of least resistance, least effort and, most of all, least responsibility. Cut to the chase, "gimme the cash" and to hell with the long term effects.

2. Righteousness or Innocence is typical to all living creatures – they have no sense of so-called "sin" or wickedness. Please remember that our source ballad for the tradition stems from the medieval period and, therefore, adjust your perceptions accordingly! This Path is described as being beset with thorns and briars because it is so difficult for humans. But, as you all know from faery tales and legends, living creatures pass in and out of the Thorny Way easily ... that is why we work with them as magical allies, for *they can go where we may not*. At least, not as isolated humans who are bound by time. The connections between Thorns and Innocence were incorporated early into Christian iconography and myth, deriving directly from pagan tradition.

3. The Path to Elfland is also called the Bonny Middle Way. Not, I should add, in the sense of equilibrium (or, in today's prescription culture, perhaps we might say equi-Valium), but in the sense that it passes in-between the two extreme paths and leads to another realm of consciousness and being: the Faery Realm, Elfland, the place of Earth Light.

These Three Roads provide clues to a process of magical transformation and spiritual maturity which I have termed, in several publications, the Threefold Alliance, a process whereby a complete being on Earth is a harmonious fusion of Human, Living Creature and Faery. The isolated human, bootstrapping himself/herself into superior awareness is a monster ... the superman of Nietzsche or the superhuman Masters of occult fiction. Indeed, it is this very foul concept of human superiority that has led us to this 21st century of pollution, disease, failing resources, and an abused and depleted planet that cannot, and will not, support us for much longer.

Of course, Thomas and the Queen have come down a path from the outer Scotland to the UnderWorld, to reach the Triple Crossroads; so a fussy person could well argue that this is a fourth way. As indeed it is ... the way through the UnderWorld that leaves human time-bound consciousness behind. It is the Dissolving Way, for as you travel it, it vanishes behind you. When you return within the transformed prophetic consciousness of the Threefold Alliance, you return by a Shortened Way, for you are no longer bound by time and space as you were before.

THE RIVERS OF BLOOD AND TEARS

To reach the Crossroads, Thomas and the Queen of Elfland pass into a mountain (in Scotland this is identified with the Eildon Hills in the Lowlands). From there they wade through Rivers of Blood and Tears. In some versions of the ballad, the Queen says that all the blood shed Above flows down into the UnderWorld, as do all the tears shed Above.

This is of great interest and potential to anyone seeking to understand and practice transformative UnderWorld/Faery magic. Let us explore it further, for it does not appear gratuitously in the folkloric ballad ... it has ancient precedents.

The two rivers are described as being of blood and tears ... blood and water, bodily fluids. They are, of course, the red and white colors of ancestral magical tradition, the third traditional color being black, or sometimes green.

The *Thomas Rhymer* material can be dated historically to source texts, and to a historical person, Thomas himself, in the 13th century. There is a long Romance poem that describes the UnderWorld journey in medieval English, attributed to Thomas[6]. We must be clear, however, that the poetic and prophetic historical texts by Thomas Earlston, Lord Learmont, are not within the genus of traditional folkloric ballads describing an UnderWorld Initiation by the Faery Queen. Such folkloric ballads were preserved in oral tradition in Scotland, along with a group of stories about Thomas, well into the 20th century. They were sung and told by people who had no knowledge of medieval literature and, in many cases, could not read or write. Somehow, an oral anonymous initiatory tradition has survived independently of literature, though attached, significantly, to a historical person.

The red and white rivers are found in other sources, of course. If we hop gracefully back in time to the 12th century, we find these red and white powers described in another invaluable source text, the Welsh (bardic) *Prophecies of Merlin*, set into Latin by Geoffrey of Monmouth but deriving from oral Welsh tradition. The boy Merlin (not the wise old man who is a product of modern fiction) has a vision of two dragons, Red and White. They rise up from a lake hidden in a cavern beneath a mountain and fight. Thereafter, the power of their interaction gives rise to the *future history* of Britain, which the boy Merlin perceives (while weeping the *tears of prophecy*) and then recites. It concludes with a cosmic apocalyptic vision that seems to synchronize with the first third of this century, the 21st CE. (Remember to stick a note on your computer screen … apocalypse coming soon!).

Setting aside the Prophecies which I have discussed in *Merlin, The Prophetic Vision and Mystic Life*[7], the significant content for us, in this article, is that of the Red and White Dragons. They embody interaction, polarity and powers that arise from the UnderWorld to the surface, thereby causing changes.

We sense a connection to the Rivers of Blood and Tears, to the red and white colors, to polarity perhaps, but what is it?

For the answer we can skip gracefully to a much earlier source text, that of Plato's *Republic*[8]. This contains one of the most significant initiatory and metaphysical expositions of the Western spiritual traditions. It is often called the legend of Er the Arminian, or Er, son of Arminius. Er dies, as it seems, and just as his body is about to be burned on the funeral pyre, he awakens and tells everyone about his experiences in the realms between death and rebirth. This is a remarkable text and shame on you if you have not read it and meditated upon it! As an aside, it describes, in just one part, the proportional orbits of the planets so accurately that Johannes Kepler (1571-1630) used it as the basis for his astronomical calculations. But we are concerned with something else, which I will paraphrase here, for sake of brevity.

Plato describes two streams of souls, one stream descending from the stars, another arising from the Earth. They pass through the UnderWorld and they intersect at the entrance thereto, in certain caverns, where they dialogue with one another. An ascending stream of souls (today we might say of consciousness) and a descending stream.

So we have: Rivers of Blood and Tears in the hollow hills (folkloric faery tradition), red and white dragons in the hollow mountain of Dinas Emrys (Welsh bardic tradition), and ascending and descending Rivers of Souls that pass through the UnderWorld and reach to the cosmos, in Plato's initiatory exposition, the story of Er (*The Republic*). These are all presentations, in tradition, of what Dion Fortune once termed the Involutionary and Evolutionary waves or streams[9]. This concept is found in several places in Dion Fortune's writings and, of course, in the lectures of Rudolph Steiner. However, it did not originate with Steiner and we must remember that the older traditions have taught it, in various forms, for thousands of years. Each generation makes its own definition or exposition, but the roots are deep within the perennial wisdom tradition.

One streams flows into the planet, one stream flows out. We might think, in modern terms, that these are the metaphysical equivalents of the forces radiated out and in, between Earth, the Solar System, and the cosmos. The folkloric traditions assert that we can initiate change within ourselves by encountering these forces directly in the UnderWorld. Plato asserts that they are essential to the processes of death and rebirth and are part of a cosmic movement that is held within the solar system.

Just like Thomas Rhymer or the prophetic child Merlin, we have to wade through these two rivers, to be permeated by the power of these two dragons, and to come into a transformed awareness. Plato describes the cosmic or long path … that of many cycles of lives.

Merlin describes how the forces create what we think of as "history" through complex interactions in the surface world, while the faery tradition reminds us that the power flows in our blood and bodily fluids. Cosmic forces, collective interactions, and individual sexuality and fertility – the Rivers of Blood and Seed, Red and White.

The Tree of Life in the UnderWorld

As mentioned above in the ballad of *Thomas Rhymer*, the Queen of Elfland reveals a Tree to Thomas Rhymer. It grows, according to tradition, at the center of the Crossroads in the UnderWorld. She tells him that all the plagues of the world above (in some versions, all the plagues of Hell) are in the fruit of this tree. Thomas is expressly forbidden to pick this fruit. Hmm ... sounds familiar, does it not?

This brief but telling reference in Scottish faery tradition is paralleled by many traditions worldwide, including esoteric themes such as the legend of the Garden of Eden and the Tree of Knowledge, as well as the redemptive story of the Tree of Life and the Ship of Solomon found in certain medieval Grail texts[10]

In most modern texts on Qabalah, in English and dating from the 19th century to the present day, we find that the Tree of Life has, apparently, no roots. Or if it does have roots, they are called the "Negative Shells," and are bad, bad, *bad,* and you must have nothing to do with them! This is similar, is it not, to the prohibition uttered in the ancient Scottish ballad? When something is tabooed, for no apparent reason, be suspicious of the reasons for its taboo.

Of course, in 19th and 20th century occultism the reason for the taboo is simple (and, to be fair, understandable) ignorance, with one writer copying from the other, laboring under Christian sexual suppression. Eventually we reach modern neo-occult journalism, where anyone can cut and paste anything into a book without understanding or practicing it. Entire publishing houses thrive on such impoverished journalism, though we must all pay lip-service to the idea that this is a good thing, as it supposedly expands the collective awareness of spirituality.

As syphilitic addicted Freud proposed long ago, it is, at least superficially, all about sex. But unlike the prurient interest of the early psychologists, or the self-indulgent pseudo-liberation of popularized so-called "tantra" (only vaguely connected with the many and varied tantric traditions of the East), we are interested here in the sexual forces as sacred, transformative and magical powers. The roots of the Tree of Life are in the UnderWorld, just as the roots of trees in nature are in the Sacred Earth. The prohibition regarding roots, in Qabalistic tradition, arises from a secret (oral) teaching that the root forces may be aroused through sexual union or, more accurately, by methods that are *similar* to sexual union, or which result in the radiance of subtle forces such as those triggered by sexual union.

By the time the text-snipping journalistic modern writers get hold of this idea of the roots of the Tree of Life and its hidden nourishment in the UnderWorld, they do not have access to the oral tradition, still found in highly secretive Jewish mystical practices. Furthermore the 19th century occultists, from whom most modern writers copy, were deeply ingrained with the childish, but powerful, notion that the UnderWorld (Hell) is evil, so any UnderWorld part of the Tree of Life must be bad for you; just as sex is bad, evil, wicked, and so forth. Conclusion? Repudiate all Roots. Ho Hum, we say. Let not the evil carrot or turnip turn you aside from sanctimony.

During the Crossroads phase of the UnderWorld Initiation, the Faery Queen shows Thomas a Tree and tells him that the fruit is poisonous, containing the plagues of the upper world, or of Hell. There follows a curious episode in which she gives him bread and wine and *he lays his head in her lap*. Those of you who have read Shakespeare's Hamlet (the mad dialogues with Ophelia) will remember that this is a sexual euphemism. Only at the foot of the UnderWorld Tree, only after partaking of bread and wine, and only after laying his head in the lap of the Queen of Elfland, is Thomas shown the vision of the Crossroads, and the way to Elfland.

Bread and wine are the transmuted substances of the fruit, of plants, and (as we all know from both ancient pagan and less ancient Christian tradition) are the body and blood ... think of the two rivers, two dragons, and two streams of souls. Blood and Water, Blood and Seed.

While it is indeed possible to understand such motifs as deriving from a physical sexual magic, we must remember that this is about union between human and nonhuman beings. It is sex Jim, but not as we know it. It may seem like sex to the modern, post-Christian individual human, but to the other orders of spiritual life, such as the faery races, it is communication, exchange and transformation. Which is, of course, what sex should be: communication, radiant with love.

The Return and the Future

UnderWorld spirituality is not an escapist path. Just as Thomas returns to the mortal world after seven years in Elfland, so does the UnderWorld initiate return to the responsibilities of the surface life ... not as a slave, but as a free man or woman.

The return path is a Shortened Way ... leading directly from the transformative realms of the UnderWorld to the outer or surface consciousness. Thomas does not retrace his steps and undo the wonders that he has experienced; he comes back as a prophet, with the tongue that cannot lie, and is shod and cloaked in green, the color of Nature.

What could be more appropriate for us now than to go to the Crossroads, to wade the Rivers of Blood and Tears, and sleep to gain visions of truth at the foot of the UnderWorld Tree, living as we do in a world that is under threat of destruction by humanity hell-bent upon the rank path of Wickedness?

Near the beginning of this article, I wrote that the Crossroads come first and last. Indeed so, at birth and at death, and in processes of magical and spiritual transformation. This 21st century is a crossroads time for humanity. Only by renewing our conscious participation in the living foundation of Earth will we be able find the way, the path, the next journey.

Endnotes

1. *The UnderWorld Initiation*, Stewart, R.J. Aquarian Press, Wellingborough, 1985, various editions (UK, USA) Mercury Publishing, Lake Toxaway, NC, 1997 (USA).

2. *Earth Light* and *Power Within the Land,* Stewart, R.J. Element Books, Shaftesbury, 1991/92 (UK, USA) Mercury Publishing, Lake Toxaway, N.C., 1997 (USA). *The Well of Light* (Book and CD) Stewart, R.J. Muse Press, Coral Springs, FL, USA.

3. Examples of such threshold texts are: *The Book of Invasions, The Mabinogion, The Prophecies* and *Life of Merlin*, the British, Irish and European vernacular (magical) ballads, collected folk and faery tales, and so forth. Many editions and collections of each may be found.

4. Crossroads magic is found widely in European faery tradition, in Voudun in the Southern USA, in blues music initiations, and many more examples.

5. See http://www.shakespeare-online.com/playanalysis/macbeth.html for a classic analysis of the play.

6. See this excellent short outline: http://www.electricscotland.com/history/other/rymer_thomas.htm

7. *Merlin, the Prophetic Vision and Mystic Life*, Stewart, R.J. Penguin Arkana, Harmondsworth, 1990. A free version of the *Prophecies* with interpretation is available at www.dreampower.com .

8. See: http://classics.mit.edu/Plato/republic.11.x.html

9. *The Cosmic Doctrine,* Fortune, Dion. Aquarian Press, Wellingborough, and other editions.

10. *The Quest of the Holy Grail,* Matarasso, PM. Penguin Classics

Thomas Rhymer

(from Scottish vernacular tradition)

See also *The English and Scottish Popular Ballads* by Frances James Child, for known texts with scholarly notes.

True Thomas lay on grassy bank
and he beheld a lady gay
a lady that was brisk and bold
to come riding o'er the ferny brae.

Her skirt was of the grass-green silk
her mantle of the velvet fine
and on every lock of her horse's mane
hung fifty siller bells and nine.

True Thomas he took of his hat
and bowed him low down to his knee
"All hail thou Virgin Queen of Heaven
for thy like on Earth I ne'er did see."

"Oh no, oh no, true Thomas" she cried
"that name does not belong to me,
for I am the queen of faire Elfland
that's come for tae visit here with thee."

And Thomas ye maun gae wi' me
True Thomas ye maun gae wi' me
An' you maun serve me seven long years
thro' weal or woe as may chance to be."

She's mounted on the milk white steed
and took true Thomas up ahind
and aye whene'er the bridel rang
the steed flew faster than the wind.

For forty days and forty nights
they wad thro' red blude to the knee
and they saw neither sun nor moon
but heard the roaring of the sea.

For forty days and forty nights
they wade thro' red blude to the knee
for all the blood that's shed here above
lights down thro' the streams of that countrie.

The saw neither sun nor moon
but heard the roaring of the sea
for all the tears that's shed here above
light down thro' the streams of that countrie.

They rade on and further on
'til they came unto a tree:
"Oh light ye doon ye lady faire
and I'll pull o' that fruit for thee."

"Oh no, oh no, true Thomas" she said
"that fruit may not be pu'd by thee
for all the plagues of the world above
light down on the fruit of this countrie"

"But I have bread here in my lap
likewise a bottle of red wine
and ere that we go further on
ye sall rest, and ye sall dine."

When he'd eaten and dranken his fill
she said "lay your head doon on my knee,
and ere we climb yon high high hill
I'll show ye wonders three…

See ye not that narrow narrow way
beset with thorns and briars?
That is the path of righteousness
Tho after it few inquires.

See ye not that broad broad way
that winds aboot the lilly leven?
That is the path of rank wickedness
tho some teach you it is the road tae he'en.

And see ye not the bonny bonny way
that winds aboot the ferny brae?
Oh that is the path tae fair Elfland
where ye and I maun gae.

True Thomas ye must hold your tongue
whate'er ye chance tae hear or see
and ye will serve me seven long yeer
thro' weel or woe as may chance tae be."

And he has gotten a coat of woven cloth
likewise the shoes of velvet green
Until seven years were past and gone
True Thomas ne'er on earth was seen.

Appendix 2:
ORCHIL

by Fiona MacLeod

From* The Silence of Amor, *1902

I dreamed of Orchil, the dim goddess who is under the brown earth, in a vast cavern, where she weaves at two looms. With one hand she weaves life upward through the grass; with the other she weaves death downward through the mould; and the sound of the weaving is Eternity, and the name of it in the green world is Time. And, through all, Orchil weaves the weft of Eternal Beauty, that passeth not, though its soul is Change.

This is my comfort, O Beauty that art of Time, (I) who am faint and hopeless in the strong sound of that other weaving, where Orchil, the dim goddess, sits dreaming at her loom under the brown earth.

Fiona Macleod (William Sharp) is a writer and mystic whose work contains a vast wealth of hidden esoteric imagery and metaphysics. While it is usually thought of as romantic "Celtic Twilight" poetry, it is founded upon Sharp's magical disciplines and received inner teachings and impulses. If we stay on the romantic Celtic surface, then it works very well at that level. But anyone with knowledge and understanding of the Western esoteric tradition can find much more in Fiona Macleod. Curiously, the deeper we go into the material, the less "Celtic" it becomes. The Celtic mode is used as a mythic gateway of images and stories that leads into a deeper consciousness wherein spiritual truths are explored. And this, of course, is how all mythology should be employed.

This meditation, quoted in full above, is especially apt as an appendix for our Cord work, as it explores the same themes as our major cord forms, such as weaving life and death, discovering continuity beyond time, and being flexible to change. It also reaches from the UnderWorld to the Solar World, and describes the twin streams of Evolution and Involution. All in three sentences, with a fourth as a coda or conclusion.

Orchil is a prose poem from the collection of meditations *The Silence of Amor*, and through this short text Fiona Macleod offers a vision of the UnderWorld Weaver Goddess. She calls this goddess Orchil, creating a "Celtic" myth which she also employs in other texts, such as *The Awakening of Angus Og*. Orchil is a place name found in Scotland, and is also the name of a violet dye obtained from lichen and used in traditional Scottish weaving and coloring. From this weaving and coloring connection Fiona/William extrapolates Orchil as the ancient Weaver goddess of the ancestral world.

The meditational visionary prose poem is concentrated and highly focused. It contains an entire metaphysical philosophical perspective on the cosmos that relates both to Qabalistic tradition and to the concepts of Einstein's relativity theory and later quantum physics. This should not be surprising, as Fiona/William was a trained esotericist who had worked ritual with W.B. Yeats and many other luminaries of the era. Additionally, the triple weaving concept found in Orchil is also expressed as the three rays of the Awen in Welsh bardic cosmology, something that Fiona/William would have been familiar with from the contemporary revival of mystical Druidism during his/her lifetime. So while there are conceptual metaphysical comparisons both backward in time, to medieval Welsh bardic texts and Qabalistic tradition, and forward beyond Fiona/William's lifespan into relativity theory and quantum physics, these are neither "sources" nor "predictions."

In Orchil, the seeress and poet offers us a spiritual vision that derives from that same realm of consciousness that inspired the druids, bards, Qabalists and physicists. In other words, it describes something that exists, that can be modeled in many different ways. This something is the interaction of Time, Space and Movement that is the woven fabric of the cosmos. It was understood as such by the philosophers of the ancient cultures, just as well as it is mathematically modeled by our contemporary physicists. It cannot be newly "discovered" because it already *Is*, yet we discover it afresh in every lifetime when we reach beyond the time-bound personality and come into the greater awareness.

> *I dreamed of Orchil the dim goddess who is under the brown earth in vast cavern, where she weaves at two looms. With one hand she weaves life upward through the grass; with the other she weaves death downwards through the mould.*

Orchil is envisioned in a vast cavern, as an UnderWorld weaver goddess. In this context, as mentioned above, she is an embodiment of the ancestral goddess known in many cultures by many names – the weaver of life and death. But the imagery is most specific: she weaves life upwards through the grass and death downwards through the mould. This image refers to the Evolutionary and Involutionary movements, often called the Streams or Rivers that pass into and out of the body of our planet Earth, and the manner in which they affect the world of nature. The upward movement, from the planetary core to the surface and then radiating off-planet to the solar system, to the cosmos, gives rise on Earth to life-forms in nature (upward through the grass). The downward movement, from the cosmos, the solar system, the sub-lunar world, towards the planetary core, strips away form and draws consciousness towards its source (downward through the mould). Mould in this context is compost, the rich layer of decomposing organic matter that is fed by dying forms and in turn feeds the green world of nature.

> *And the sound of the weaving is Eternity, and the name of it in the green world is Time.*

With this line the author reveals another level to the twofold movement, and takes us from the cycles of life and death in nature, into the relationship between manifest existence on Earth (the green world) and the cosmos (eternity). From the upward and downward movements, we are taken to two sacro-magical concepts: the *sound* of the weaving and the *name* of it.

The Sound of the Weaving

Let us first consider the sound. All sound arises from energetic interaction. There has to be an interaction of *movement* to generate a sound wave (one force interacting with another, typically such as the energy applied by a bow to a violin string, or the energy applied to a speaker cone by an electrical signal). In this case the interaction and movement is that of the two looms: the Evolutionary upward movement and the Involutionary downward movement. They generate a *sound*.

This image leads us into a wealth of associations with the mythology and the metaphysics of the ancient world. Anyone with a classical education, such as William/Fiona and his/her readers, would immediately be reminded of the famous passage in Plato's *Republic* where the goddess Arete spins the spindle of the cosmos, making a twined cord for weaving. As she does so, the three Fates, Clotho, Atropos and Lachesis, each utter a sound, a tone that resonates of the future, the present and the past.

Clotho ("spinner") was said to be the youngest of the Fates, who spun the thread of life. Her Roman equivalent was *Nona*, "the Ninth," who was originally a goddess called upon in the ninth month of pregnancy. Thus, she is also of the future. The Ninth is the number of the Moon and the sub-lunar world defined by the Moon interacting with Earth. The future of manifest life in nature is imprinted in the sub-lunar world, a theme that we have discussed at length in our main chapters.

Lachesis ("drawer of lots") measured the thread of life with her rod. Her Roman equivalent was *Decima* (the "Tenth"). Thus, she is also of the present, for life is always lived in the present with no knowledge of its measure. The Tenth is the world of our planet Earth, and likewise the manifest Kingdom of the Tree of Life which is all manifest matter in the cosmos. The present is that of manifestation into time and form.

Atropos ("inexorable") cuts the thread of life with her shears. She chose the manner of a person's death. Thus she is of the past for, with her shears, the story ends, the manifest form ceases, and the imprint of the sub-lunar world fades. The deeper spiritual entity that has manifested in form withdraws into the solar world, prior to rebirth.

Fiona Macleod has drawn upon the rich classical sources of the Fates and the esoteric tradition (in Plato) that the life cycle of the individual and of the planets of the solar system are all uttered as tones or sounds. In many creation myths, it is a sound, a word or an utterance that defines cosmos out of chaos, the universe out of the void.

The Name of the Weaving

The sound of Orchil's weaving is Eternity, but the name of it in the green world is Time. Eternity becomes Time at the bottom of the well … in this case the gravity well. For Fiona/William, the "green world" and "green life" described the word of nature, but included much of the spiritual world of nature, and was by no means limited to manifest forms.

Thus, we have an upwards weaving of life, a downwards weaving of death, and the sound of eternity which we can hear, apparently arising out of their movement and interaction. But in fact, it is the upward and downward movements that arise out of the Sound of Eternity. While we are in the green world entangled by Time, we sense only the polarized twin movements of Life and Death and cannot grasp that they are sourced out of Eternity. For us the weaving is defined and named as Time, for this is how we relate to Evolution and Involution, to life and death.

The Weft of the Weaving

And, through all, Orchil weaves the weft of Eternal Beauty, that passeth not, though its soul is Change.

In weaving, the weft is the cross-thread, the horizontal that ties together the vertical strands. Thus, Eternal Beauty ties together Life and Death, Eternity and Time. Here Fiona/William is employing Qabalistic and Platonic concepts, for the 6th Sphere of the Tree of Life, which is called Beauty or Harmony, has the Sun as its manifest vessel and all center-points wherever they occur. Upon the Tree of Life, the Sun is at the center and holds everything together. Just as the physical star, our Sun, is at the center of the Solar System. Beauty, Balance, Harmony and Centrality: this is the weft of Eternal Beauty.

Next comes a significant spiritual truth: eternal beauty passes not, though its soul is Change. We might liken this, in a physical analogy, to the flexibility of the weft that can change into any shape as the cloth is worn, bundled, folded and moved. The weft holds the cloth together in Balance; it is not rigid or fixed, it passes not, yet it can change into an infinite variety of shapes. This is the interaction of Time, Space and Movement that is found both in mysticism and in relativity theory.

This is my comfort, O Beauty that art of Time, (I) who am faint and hopeless in the strong sound of that other weaving, where Orchil, the dim goddess, sits dreaming at her loom under the brown earth.

This coda to the main vision deals with the mystery of spiritual consolation: *this is my comfort, O Beauty that art of Time* and, in the deeper sacro-magical arts, that of grace.

Often the human soul and mind feels entrapped by the inexorable weaving of the Fates, of the two looms of Orchil, of the Evolutionary and Involutionary streams. Yet, we also have an inherent sense of the higher octaves of creation, where beauty and grace indicate to us that there is Eternity as the source of the Weaving. Note that Orchil is *dreaming* at her looms: her dream of creation and destruction flows through all life on earth. By grasping the weft, that other strand that holds the weaving together, we are able to come into the realm of Eternal Beauty. Paradoxically, it is our bondage into time that enables us to distinguish that there is freedom beyond time.

Printed in the United States
64757LVS00003B/85-168